CW00351180

COST AND MANAGEMENT ACCOUNTING

Trevor Daff

Pitman

Pitman Publishing
128 Long Acre, London WC2E 9AN

A Longman Group Company

First published 1988

© Longman Group UK Limited 1988

A CIP catalogue record for this book is available from the British Library

ISBN 0–273–02983–5

All rights reserved; no part of this publication may be reproduced,
stored in a retrieval system, or transmitted in any form or by any other
means, electronic, mechanical, photocopying, recording, or otherwise, without
either the prior written permission of the Publishers or a licence permitting
restricted copying in the United Kingdom issued by the Copyright Licensing
Agency, 33–34 Alfred Place, London WC1E 7DP. This book may not be lent,
resold, hired out or otherwise disposed of by way of trade or in any
form of binding or cover other than that in which it is
published, without the prior consent of the publishers.

Printed in Great Britain at The Bath Press, Avon

Contents

Acknowledgements

We are grateful to the Financial Times for permission to reproduce an extract from *Financial Times* 8/3/83 and the following examination boards for questions from past examination papers: Association of Accounting Technicians; The Association of Cost & Executive Accountants; The Chartered Association of Certified Accountants; The Chartered Institute of Management Accountants; The Institute of Cost and Management Accountants; The London Chamber of Commerce; The Royal Society of Arts Examinations Board; University of London School Examinations Board

and to the following for illustrative material:

Cambridgeshire County Council for Figs. 6.3 and 12.2; The Chartered Institute of Management Accountants for Figs. 10.1, 11.3 and Table 14.3; The Controller of Her Majesty's Stationery Office for Fig. 3.2 and Table 2.1 "Crown Copyright"; Howard Shinn Printing for Fig. 7.1; The London Borough of Tower Hamlets for Fig. 3.1; Pegasus Software Limited for Fig. 8.1.

Any answers or hints on answers are the sole responsibility of the author and have not been provided or approved by the examination boards. The examination boards accept no responsibility for the accuracy or method of working in any of the answers.

The author is indebted to Janet Hackett for her help and secretarial services, and to Geoff Black for his useful advice.

Chapter 1

Courses and syllabuses

This book seeks to help those whose studies include at least some element of *Cost and Management Accounting*. This may be the case if you are following a GCE 'A' Level accounting course or a course leading to the award of a certificate of the London Chamber of Commerce, the Pitman Examinations Institute, or the Royal Society of Arts. Alternatively, your course might be for a business studies award from BTEC or SCOTVEC or it might be a component of the examinations of one of the professional accounting or commercial bodies. Or again you may be following a general management course which contains elements of *Cost and Management Accounting*. You may be attending college full-time, part-time day, or on an evening course; or you may be using distance learning packages, or material from a correspondence college. Irrespective of the qualification aimed for, or your mode of study, if your studies include *Cost and Management Accounting* as a component, then this book should help in your revision throughout the year and in your preparations for the final examinations.

The book examines not only the accounting methods in common use, but it also discusses the principles which lie behind these methods. The role of *Cost and Management Accounting* as an aid to the management function is never forgotten.

The chapter topics have been chosen to reflect current syllabuses and examination papers. The questions used to illustrate the chapters have been taken from recent examination papers, and where possible, the comments of examiners upon candidates' performance have been incorporated in the text.

It has clearly not been possible to select questions from all relevant accounting examination bodies: the questions selected are to be seen as representative of those currently being set. Examination questions from the following examination bodies have been used:

- Association of Accounting Technicians (AAT);
- Association of Cost and Executive Accountants (ACEA);
- Chartered Association of Certified Accountants (ACCA/CACA);
- Chartered Institute of Management Accountants (CIMA);
- London Chamber of Commerce (LCC);
- Royal Society of Arts (RSA);
- University of London Schools Examinations Board (ULSEB).

The following Syllabus Coverage Chart acts as a guide to the major topics covered in the book, relating them to the relevant syllabuses. *The chart should be used only as a guide*. Syllabuses are open to interpretation, and each year syllabuses may be modified in terms of content and emphasis. Do check against an up-to-date copy of the syllabus for your particular examination.

SYLLABUS COVERAGE CHART

TOPIC	GCE 'A' Level	LCC Inter	LCC Higher	RSA I	RSA II	RSA III	AA I Part 2	ACEA Level 3
Nature and scope	✓	✓	✓	✓	✓	✓	✓	✓
Material costs	✓	✓	✓	✓	✓	✓	✓	✓
Labour costs	✓	✓	✓	✓	✓	✓	✓	✓
Overheads: collection, classification, allocation	✓	✓	✓	✓	✓	✓	✓	✓
Overheads: apportionment to production	✓	✓	✓	✓	✓	✓	✓	✓
Batch and job costing	✓	✓	✓	✓	✓	✓	✓	✓
Contract costing	✓	✓	✓	✓	✓	✓	✓	✓
Process costing	✓	✓	✓	✓	✓	✓	✓	✓
Service costing		✓	✓	✓	✓	✓		✓
Absorption and marginal costing	✓	✓	✓	✓	✓	✓	✓	✓
Budgets and budgetary control	✓		✓			✓	✓	✓
Cash budgets and master budgets	✓		✓	✓		✓	✓	✓
Std costing: labour and materials	✓		✓		✓	✓	✓	✓
Std costing: overheads	✓		✓		✓	✓	✓	✓
Investment appraisal	✓						✓	✓

AIA	AAT	CIMA CAC	CIMA MAT	ICSA	Institute of Chartered Accountants E&W	Institute of Chartered Accountants SCOTLAND	SCCA I	SCCA III	BTEC National	SCOTVEC National	ACCA CMA I
√	√	√		√	√	√	√	√	√	√	√
√	√			√	√				√	√	√
√	√			√	√		√	√	√	√	√
√	√	√		√	√	√	√		√	√	√
√	√	√		√	√	√	√	√	√	√	√
√	√	√		√	√	√	√	√	√	√	√
√	√	√		√		√	√	√	√	√	√
√	√	√		√	√	√	√	√	√	√	√
√			√			√	√				
√	√	√	√	√		√	√	√	√	√	√
√	√	√		√	√	√	√	√	√	√	√
√	√	√	√	√	√	√	√	√	√	√	√
√	√	√	√	√	√	√	√	√	√	√	√
√	√	√	√	√	√	√	√	√	√	√	√
√	√		√		√	√			√	√	√

Chapter 2

Examination techniques

Many candidates who have clearly worked diligently during their course fail to earn the examination pass merited by their efforts simply because they have not given any thought to their examination technique. The following comments are aimed at removing this deficiency, and at allowing those students who have worked well to obtain maximum benefit from their endeavours.

The type of examination you sit will vary depending upon the examination body concerned. There will be differences in the *time allowed* per paper – usually 2, 2½ or 3 hours; in the *structure* of the paper, such as the number of questions to be attempted, the choice of questions available, the presence or absence of compulsory questions, and the mark allocation. Your tutor should explain these details to you well in advance of the examination date, but do take care to check for *yourself*. Make sure that you fully understand the nature and form of your examination. The following check-list may prove useful:

- Examining body
- Syllabus to be examined
- Weighting of topics
- Date of examination
- Location
- Duration of examination
- Structure of the paper
- Number of questions to be attempted
- Mark allocation
- Date and form for announcing results

LEVELS OF LEARNING

In any but the most elementary examinations, the examiners will seek to test various levels of learning in a balanced manner; and the levels they test will help to determine the types of questions you will be set.

KNOWLEDGE

The lowest level of *learning* has to do with simple *memory*. Questions testing *knowledge* seek to discover whether the candidate is aware of, and can recall, the fundamental elements of the subject. This might include knowledge of terminology, which forms the basic language of the subject, or of facts; knowledge of ways of organising data into conventional forms; knowledge of conventions, of usages, and of acceptable styles; knowledge of categories and classifications, of principles, and theories.

In Cost and Management Accounting, knowledge of specific terms and definitions is crucially important, and students are advised at the earliest time to obtain and to read the latest edition of *Management Accounting: Official Terminology* published by the Chartered Institute of Management Accountants, 63 Portland Place, London W1N 4AB.

Knowledge of the conventional presentation of accounting information, of conventional styles and acceptable layouts is also important, and should be carefully learned.

COMPREHENSION

The lowest level of *understanding* has to do with the interpretation and extrapolation of facts, terms, and principles. This level of learning can be tested by presenting information to candidates, and asking them to submit it in a different form, such as re-drafting an accounting statement. Again it can be tested by asking candidates to interpret a message provided in technical language, or to extrapolate from given data so that trends or predictions can be derived.

Comprehension is also tested by asking you to make *inferences* from the data or situation presented. This may involve simplifying the data or deriving consequences, corollaries, and effects in accordance with the information given. An example would be changing a materials issued statement from a system based on FIFO to one based on AVCO, and showing the effect upon recorded profits.

APPLICATION

The next level of understanding concerns the remembering – and the bringing to bear upon given material – of appropriate generalisations or principles. Here we are concerned with the use of abstractions in concrete situations, such as problem solving when an appropriate method is not suggested. An example of this is where you are asked to give advice to a firm which is concerned that two identical jobs for the same customer have accumulated different amounts of cost, largely because of the way in which overheads are recovered. (Standard costing?)

5

ANALYSIS

In *comprehension*, the emphasis is upon the grasp of the meaning of the material: in *application*, it is upon remembering and bringing to bear upon given material the appropriate generalisations and principles. *Analysis* seeks to test an ability to distinguish fact from hypothesis; to identify conclusions and supporting statements; to distinguish relevant from extraneous material; to note how one idea relates to another; to see what unstated assumptions are involved in what is said.

Analysis therefore involves the breaking down of material into its constituent parts, the detecting of relationships between the parts, and an appreciation of the way in which they are organised. Questions under this heading sometimes take the form of a lengthy statement, followed by questions relating to the statement.

SYNTHESIS

This involves *putting together* the elements and parts so as to form a whole. It is a process of combining elements in such a way as to constitute a pattern or a structure which was not clearly visible before, and which is more than the sum of the materials the candidate began to work with.

The scope for creative expression here is great. However, it is bounded by limits set by the problem, and by the theoretical or methodological framework. A problem involving *synthesis* will also require skills in all of the previous levels of learning.

Planning a field study for assignment work, or specifying the conduct of an investigative works' visit, may be examples here, especially where candidates are asked to communicate those plans to other people in a group. An ability to report effectively upon personal experiences regarding the field trip or the visit is a useful indication that the candidate can synthesise material.

EVALUATION

Finally, *evaluation* concerns the *making of judgements* about the materials and methods for given purposes. These may involve quantitative and qualitative judgements about the extent to which materials and methods satisfy particular criteria. It is at this final level of learning that personal values, likings, etc. have a part to play.

Questions here have to do with comparing major theories, or with recognising and evaluating the different values involved in different courses of action. An assessment of the way in which Cost and Management Accounting supports the profit motive may be an example here.

TYPES OF QUESTION

The *level* of learning which the examiner is seeking to test, as well as the *nature* of the subject matter, will determine the *type* of question set: Table 2.1 indicates the characteristics of various types of question. Most examination papers will contain a variety of questions. However where multiple choice (or objective test) questions are used, they usually appear on a separate paper, or as a separate section within a paper, since strict timing is important for such questions.

Table 2.1

Characteristic	Type of question		
	Multiple choice	Short answer	Essay
Measure of:			
Factual knowledge	Medium	Most	Least
Reasoning	Most	Least	Medium
Verbal ability	Least	Medium	Most
Pure subject	Medium	Most	Least
Creativity	Least	Medium	Most
Coverage of subject material	Good	Medium	Poor
Susceptibility to guessing	Most	Medium	Least

Source: *Manual of Trade Proficiency Testing*: RAF, 1968.

COMPUTATIONAL

Questions involving calculations may be either very short and simple – as with the calculation of a firm's breakeven output – or they may be lengthy and complex – as when producing a cash budget followed by a master budget. Numerical questions may seek to test knowledge and application of a simple formula, or they may involve the handling of quantities of data, the application of accounting principles, and the organising of data into conventional formats.

LONG ANSWER

These questions may take the form of essays, briefing papers, reports, long notes, etc. Long answer questions may require a discussion of some aspect of Cost and Management Accounting, such as a comparison of the strengths and weaknesses of non-discounting methods of investment appraisal. They may ask candidates to analyse accounting statements, to comment upon a quotation from an accounting journal, or to discuss information which has been presented in a graphical, numerical, or pictorial form.

SHORT ANSWER

Computational questions often contain an additional written element, which asks candidates to define particular terms used in the question, or to use their answer from an earlier part of the question and to evaluate or to apply it. The time allowance for these questions – and the mark allocation – is usually relatively small, but experience shows that this is where the good candidates begin to score.

MULTIPLE CHOICE

Sometimes, these are called *objective test* questions. They usually consist of a short statement which sets the problem, followed by up to four suggested answers. Candidates are asked to mark or to choose the answer which they feel is correct. Thus:

> *Which method of pricing materials issued will give the most realistic value of closing stock during periods of rising prices?*
>
> A.   AVCO   B.   FIFO   C.   LIFO

If part of your examination includes such questions, the syllabus will usually say so.

ASSIGNMENTS

Many courses have some of their assessment based upon course work. The assignments set may be similar to those covered by traditional examinations, so that the advice provided in this book will be as relevant to assignments as to examinations.

Some assignment work may seek to integrate various elements of a course, so that material covered in Statistics, Economics, and Cost and Management Accounting may all be tested in the same assignment. The approach to tackling such integrated projects is beyond the scope of this book; however, a thorough knowledge of *each* of the component subjects will be essential before integration can usefully take place. This book can help in the preparation of the Cost and Management Accounting input: other books in the series will offer similar help with other subjects.

PREPARING FOR THE EXAMINATION

The aim of particular examinations will often be given at the head of the relevant syllabus: before beginning your detailed preparation, therefore, obtain an up-to-date copy of the syllabus, and make sure that you are aware of the purpose and scope of the examination.

In any event your examination will test the various levels of learning referred to above: the *more advanced* the examination, the more likely it is that you will be tested on the higher order learning skills of *application*, *synthesis*, and *evaluation*. Evidence of your *knowledge* and *understanding* will be sought through the exercise of numerical and communication skills.

NUMERICAL SKILLS

By its very nature, Cost and Management Accounting demands that its students be basically numerate. Candidates for examinations, therefore, must be fully at ease with the manipulation of figures, through addition, subtraction, multiplication, and division. They should also be able easily to handle fractions, decimals, and percentages. If you find difficulty with any of these, it is worth setting time aside to concentrate upon them.

Many examination bodies allow candidates to use calculators in examinations, although usually the rule is that they should be non-programmable calculators. You should check carefully the regulations for your examination. If you intend to use a calculator, then ensure that you have used it extensively during revision, and that you are fully familiar with its method of operation. It is foolish to take a new, untried and strange calculator into the examination: it could have disastrous results.

Also, when using a calculator, always check the result by forming a mental estimation of the answer: it is so easy to miscalculate by placing the decimal point in the wrong place, or by pressing a wrong key. Get used to checking your calculations during revision, and it will become second nature in the examination room.

Examiners usually insist that candidates show clearly all their workings. If you are using a calculator, therefore, do ensure that you write into your script the various stages of the calculation. If you do not, and you make an error, the examiner cannot discover where you went wrong, and any marks you could have earned for the correct application of principles will have been lost. Again, if you develop this practice during revision, it will hold you in good stead in the examination.

COMMUNICATION SKILLS

Management accounting is the provision of information to management to ensure effective planning, monitoring and control. The ability of management accountants to *communicate effectively* is therefore essential. Because of this, most examinations in the subject will seek to test the candidates' abilities in written communication: papers will therefore contain *discussive* (e.g. essay) as well as computational questions. Experience shows that accounting students generally are not good at discussive questions; answers tend to be woolly, off the point, and badly planned. Time after time, examiners bemoan this fact in the examiners' reports.

If your written English is poor, then you will need to concentrate upon its improvement; spelling, punctuation, elementary grammar and style are all worthy of attention. Ensure that you know how to prepare a letter, a report, and a memo. Be clear of the meaning of requests to *define*, to *explain*, to *evaluate*, to *compare and contrast*, to *describe*, to *state*. Do not overlook the importance of communication skills in your revision programme: and get help if you need it.

REVISION

It is important that you plan your *revision* for the examination, but plan it sensibly. Candidates who plan to revise for three hours per night for the final six weeks before the examination are deluding themselves if they think that this is a sensible way to prepare. Set yourself a reasonable timetable, and make allowances for other aspects of your life. Many students find that, psychologically, Saturday evenings do not result in a very high work rate; so arrange for time off on Saturdays.

Beware, too, of long periods of revision, since diminishing

returns may set in; and never, ever, take stimulants to help you work late into the night. The side effects can be dangerous, and the quality of your work may be poor. One candidate who had revised on stimulants wrote pages and pages during the examination, and emerged well pleased with himself: in fact, he had merely written his name and address time after time.

Some students find the subject of Cost and Management Accounting relatively easy; they have to work at it, but they feel at home with the principles and ideas of the subject. Other students, equally intelligent and hardworking, find the subject more difficult. Again, some people find that they can retain information easily, whilst others do not. Discover what sort of person you are, and devise your revision plan accordingly. Do not adopt a strategy merely because it is being followed by your friends.

During your course, the *whole* of the syllabus should have been covered. With some examining bodies, the syllabus topics have weightings shown to give a guide to the depth of study required. When planning your revision, always plan to revise over the whole syllabus: it is dangerous to go question spotting, concentrating efforts on only parts of the syllabus.

Wherever possible, obtain recent copies of past examination papers for your examination: these will indicate the style of question being set and the depth of response expected. They will also confirm the structure of the paper, and enable you to become familiar with it.

Also, consult examiners' reports. Most examining bodies publish reports on their examinations some months after the examination date. The reports are written by the chief and senior examiners and are based upon the comments received from all of the examiners involved in marking the papers. The reports will indicate those areas where candidates had difficulties, and will identify major weaknesses in the scripts. By taking note of these comments, you should safeguard yourself from similar failings.

Other sources of help at this time are the various text books available. Always try to use more than one, since each author will have a different slant upon the subject. By reading more than one, you will learn to view topics from different perspectives. A topic which you find difficult to understand in one book, may become quite clear in another.

Many of the journals of the professional institutes have special sections aimed at student members: ensure that you make use of the articles here. Read the journal of your own institute, but try also to read the journal of other bodies.

Do not forget the comments made by your tutor on your own coursework. The chances are that your tutor will arrange for revision classes for you to attend. Attend these regularly, contribute to the discussions, and take the opportunity to raise any issues that still puzzle you. Do not be afraid to ask questions, no matter how basic they may be; other people in the group may have the same difficulties, and like you, be unwilling to raise them.

As your revision progresses, and the examination comes nearer, it is often useful to work on questions under examination conditions, i.e. against the clock, and without resorting to reference books. It is useful to calculate a figure for 'minutes per mark' to help assess how long to spend on a question. Assume your examination is of 3 hours' duration. Allowing 10 minutes for reading time at the beginning, and a further 10 minutes at the end for checking, there are thus 160 minutes remaining. If the paper is marked out of 100, you can afford to spend 1.6 minutes for each mark on a question. A 20-mark question therefore should receive $20 \times 1.6 = 32$ minutes. If you are still on this question after 35 minutes, you should consider leaving it and moving on: later, if you have time, you can return to the question and complete it.

Be careful to check the duration of your paper and the mark allocation: times vary from 2, 2½, to 3 hours, and mark allocations usually from 100, 120, to 150. These factors will obviously affect your 'minutes per mark' calculation.

Even if your examination is of the open book type – where you are allowed access to text and reference books – it is still worthwhile revising in the usual way. If you know your material well, you will be able to spend time in the examination showing what you know, rather than spending long periods hunting through text books.

THE EXAMINATION

Having revised fully, and become thoroughly familiar with the structure of the examination paper, there remains the examination itself.

BEFORE THE DAY OF THE EXAMINATION

Check that your examination entry is in order, that all fees have been paid, and that your candidature has been confirmed by the examining body. Usually, you will receive an official entry slip showing your unique candidate number. When you receive this, check it at once: is your name correctly spelt, have you been entered for the right examination, at the right level, on the right day, and at the proper location?

If the answer to any of these questions is 'no' then contact the relevant examinations officer, or the examining body directly. Keep your entry slip in a safe place: you may need it to gain access to the examination room.

Ensure that all the equipment you will need is ready and is put somewhere safely. Check that you have all that you may need: pens, pencils, pencil sharpener, coloured pencils, ruler, eraser, calculator. Note that many examining bodies do not allow the use of correcting fluid on scripts. Check that your pencil eraser is clean, and put new batteries in your calculator. Some calculators become unreliable if the batteries are running down. Ensure that you have sufficient pens to write your examinations. Black, blue, or blue-black inks are preferred: never use pencil or red or green ink to write your script.

Check that you know the day, time, and venue for your examination, since there may be a number of different examinations being conducted at the same time. If you have to travel to the examination, or if the examination is being held in a room you are not familiar with, take time to check the travel arrangements, and if possible, visit the room beforehand, to find out where it is and to get a 'feel' for it. There is nothing worse than arriving late for an examination because you misjudged the travelling time, or you could not find the room.

If there is likely to be any medical reason why your performance in the examination may be impaired, find out what steps you must take. Some examining bodies will allow special dispensation if they are asked well in advance, and if cases are supported by current medical evidence, such as a letter from your doctor. This may take time to organise, so do not leave it until the last minute.

If on the morning of the examination something happens to upset you – a bump in your car, or a fall from your motor cycle – do ensure that the invigilator knows about it. The circumstances can then be entered on the invigilation sheet, and the examining body informed. You can – and should – obtain supporting evidence later.

ON THE DAY OF THE EXAMINATION

Arrange for the day of the examination to be as free of stress as possible. You should have gone to bed at a reasonable time for a number of nights before the day of the examination. The knowledge that your preparation has been sound should help to keep your nerves under control. Remember, all examiners want students to do well in their papers.

Get up early on the day of the examination, and have a good bath or shower to help release the tension. Dress in comfortable clothes: there is nothing worse than undergoing an examination if your shoes are pinching.

Aim to arrive at the examination room in good time. Do not, however, congregate with large groups of other candidates; their nervousness may be catching, and could threaten to undo some of the good work you have already done. Far better to seek a little peace where you can compose yourself and collect your thoughts.

Once admitted to the examination room, you may find that a desk has been reserved for you. If not, then choose wisely; away from a window where hot sun, or strong wind may distract you; away from a door where you may be disturbed by people entering or leaving the room; in full view of the clock and the invigilator, in case you need to attract attention during the examination.

THE EXAMINATION PAPER

Once at your seat, set out your pens and equipment carefully; this will help to calm any initial nerves. Take a good look around you to familiarise yourself with the environment. The moment you have so long worked for has now come: if you have prepared soundly, you can be confident that your preparations will see you through. Do not dwell on those items which you feel you have forgotten: the chances are that when the need arises, and when you are once into your stride, the relevant knowledge will come back to you.

If there is reading time allowed in the examination, then use it sensibly. Quietly and carefully read through the question paper, perhaps making a few rough notes as you go, and underlining important aspects of each question. If there is no reading time allowed, then spend the first ten minutes or so reading the paper, and adjust your writing time accordingly.

It is easy here for all your planning to come undone, especially if candidates near to you begin writing furiously: you may feel that you too should rush pen to paper. Resist the temptation. Some students begin writing too soon, often as a reaction to nervous pressures, and the quality of their early answers is often suspect as a result.

Read the paper's rubric carefully. Check the structure of the paper to ensure that it is as you understood it to be; check the choice of questions open to you, the marks for – and thus the time you can devote to – each question. Are there any compulsory questions? How much time do these need?

Read *all* the questions. Make sure that you understand what is being asked, so that when you come to make your choice, you are fully aware of the implications. Sometimes, a question may be different from what it appears to be at first glance: make sure that you read all the questions thoroughly.

Beware, too, of misinterpreting a question: a question asking *how* a system of budgetary control should be introduced does not require an answer on the advantages of budgetary control. If the question asks *why* it is important to control waste and scrap, you are not asked to state how these items might be controlled.

Sometimes, an essay question may contain within itself more than one part: *what are the functions of management accounting,* and *how are these functions carried out*? It is essential to answer both the *what* and the *how*.

Having read the paper fully, and being aware of the choice available, you can choose your questions, and allocate the time for each based upon the marks they carry. Aim to attempt all the questions asked of you, even though you may be more confident of some than of others; and begin with what for you seems an easy question. In this way you begin by building on success, and your confidence will increase once you have one good answer under your belt. It is not necessary to begin by answering the compulsory questions.

Do not answer more questions than you are asked: you will not receive additional credit, and you will have wasted time. Some examining bodies will mark the first questions only, others will mark all questions and will select the best of those which abide by the rubric.

Keep strictly to the time you have allocated to each question: if the time expires before you have finished, leave the question at a suitable point, and go onto the next one. If you have time at the end of the examination, you can go back and complete your work. Even if you cannot, the chances are that you will have scored the majority of the marks which you are likely to score on that question.

If during the examination you have a genuine need to leave the room, do not hesitate to attract the invigilator's attention. The invigilating authorities will have made arrangements to escort people from the room, and whilst you are sitting in discomfort, your mind will be distracted from doing its best work. It is after all *your* examination.

And a warning: all examination bodies are very severe with candidates found to be or suspected of cheating. Not only will that script be void, but so might all the others taken with that examining body at that series. It is quite easy for experienced examiners to detect where cheating has gone on; and not only will the copier's script be voided, so too will the script of the candidate from whom copies were made. With some of the professional institutes, candidates caught cheating may have their registered student status suspended or removed – a sad start to a professional career. It is not worth the risk, so don't do it.

ANSWERING NUMERICAL QUESTIONS

Much of the examination in Cost and Management Accounting will involve numerical questions. With many topics you will have learned the layout of the necessary accounting statement when studying the topic. Always include the correct heading for your statement: there may be marks for this. Allow plenty of room for your working, and show your calculations clearly, even if you are using a calculator. When using the vertical presentation of accounts, it is sensible to leave sufficient room on either side of your first column of figures in case you need to extend or to indent your working. Keep all related figures underneath one another – this reduces the risk of error for you, makes any search for mistakes easier, and allows your work to be easily understood by the examiner. Use a ruler for drawing straight lines. Some examination bodies penalise untidy work; but the greatest penalty is when you are not given credit for correct work because the examiner cannot understand your script.

If you find that you have made a mistake, do not worry. If you have time to correct it within your time allocation for that question, then do so. If there is not sufficient time, then leave it. Provided that all the principles are correct, and your workings are clearly shown, you will receive credit for the principles. When altering incorrect figures, always re-write them: never alter an existing figure, since this can be doubly confusing, even to you. Once you have left a question to begin another one, concentrate upon the one in hand, and do not have your mind half on the previous question. Remember, things are never as bad – or as good – as they at first appear to be.

ANSWERING GRAPHICAL QUESTIONS

Questions requiring graphs – breakeven charts, profit graphs, Pareto curves – should be straightforward, and yet candidates often fail to score very well. Use a ruler for all lines; colour code the lines on the graph if you wish – but do not spend time uselessly producing a work of art. Clearly label all axes and all lines, identifying any points on the graph which may be particularly significant. And make your graph big enough to use. Allow a border of about 4 centimetres all around it, and use all the space available. Provide a title for the graph. Do not overburden it with too much detail: better to produce a second graph. Ensure that all measurements taken from the axes are accurate. Above all, take care to produce work which is clear and neat.

ANSWERING ESSAY QUESTIONS

Discussive answers should always be planned, no matter whether they are for short 10-minute questions, or for more detailed half hour questions. Check the question to make sure that you fully understand what is required: jot down all relevant issues you think of as they come to mind, and amplify the issues as you go. Do not attempt to arrange the material into any ordered sequence until this first *brainstorming* phase has been completed. Check back to the question all the time to ensure that only relevant material is being included. Each item in your list may become the subject of its own paragraph, leading from one to another. Once this has been done, structure the answer in terms of an introduction, the main points, and a conclusion.

The *introduction* should be brief, setting the scene for what follows by defining any technical terms, and identifying alternative lines of argument. Thus, in an essay on why it is important to control waste and scrap, the introduction may begin by distinguishing the two terms: waste is discarded substance which has no value, and scrap is discarded material which does have a recovery value.

The *body* of the answer should then flow according to your plan, the points being made concisely and in a logical sequence. Always explain technical terms when you first use them in an answer, and write terms out in full, followed by any standard abbreviation, before relying upon the short form. Be careful not to dwell too long on examples, or to go off at a tangent. Frequent reference to your plan, and to the question's wording should help to avoid this. Do, however, give examples as your answer develops: some questions will ask for examples to be given, and you will receive credit. The secret is to keep examples short and to the point.

The *conclusion* need not be very lengthy, but your answer needs to be brought to a seemly end. You may summarise briefly the main points you have made, sketching out your argument in retrospect. Some questions ask you to weigh the pros and cons and to make a decision: the conclusion is where you should finally decide, giving brief reasons and pointing out any limitations of your choice. Often, of course, there will be no one right answer, much will depend upon managerial preference and circumstance; in such situations, say so clearly. Beware of embarking upon detailed discussion in the conclusion – this should have gone on in the main body of the answer. Neither should any new material be introduced into the conclusion, otherwise your answer will simply ramble on to no purpose.

ANSWERING MULTI-CHOICE QUESTIONS

These questions will usually form a separate paper, and the examination syllabus will have warned you of what to expect. The general rule is to go through the paper once, answering all those questions which come easily to you. You can then go back and spend time studying the others. Do, however, read the questions carefully; sometimes the wording used can be deliberately confusing.

If you make a mistake, indicate it according to the rubric of the examination, and make your second choice.

I know of no examining body that penalises wrong answers, even though statistically allowances can be made for guessing. Therefore, if towards the end of the examination there are still questions you have not answered, mark in your best guesses. You will get zero if you write nothing; at least by guessing you may score. You have nothing to lose. You can usually eliminate some of the obviously wrong answers so that you have a better chance of your 'guess' being correct.

THE FINAL MINUTES

If your time allocation has been correctly calculated, and faithfully applied, you will have left yourself a few minutes at the end of the examination to read through what you have written. This is very important. With the pressure of time, and the stress of examination nerves, candidates sometimes do not always write what they mean; they may write that something is not the case, when they really mean that it is. It is not unusual to receive an answer that is internally inconsistent. Abbreviations may sometimes be transposed, with serious results: IRR may be written, when NPV was meant; an adverse variance in standard costing may be shown as being favourable. It is unwise to allow a script written under pressure to go forward to the examiner before you have had a few quiet moments to read it through yourself. This is the last chance you will have of correcting your work.

If on re-reading answers you feel that you have misread a question, leave it. So often, candidates under stress cross out perfectly good work in the mistaken belief that it is incorrect. You are not penalised for wrong answers so let it stand. With only a few minutes of the examination left, there is probably insufficient time to rework the question anyway. The final reading through is merely to check on wording, presentation, and simple calculations.

Once having read your script, collate the papers, ensuring that they are all numbered and headed according to any instructions you have been given. Check that no pages have fallen amongst rough notes or have otherwise gone astray.

AFTER THE EXAMINATION

Some students like to dwell on their examination once it is over, and this is understandable. Talking helps to throw off the tensions of enforced silence and examination pressure. But, if you have other papers still to sit, it is unwise to spend too much time conducting a post mortem. You may only distress yourself unnecessarily by wondering whether you did this or that: it cannot help the examination just ended, and it may impair your performance in those papers yet to come. Be content in the knowledge that you have done your best and be confirmed in your intent to give of your best in the papers yet to come.

IF THINGS GO WRONG

If you have followed the above advice, you should be fully able to give of your best. But sometimes, students who have prepared thoroughly find themselves faced with an examination paper which they feel unable to attempt. Usually this arises because a bout of nerves drives out all ability to analyse questions properly: panic may cause the mind to go blank.

If this should happen, *do not leave the examination room*. Sit quietly, and try to detach yourself from the examination by concentrating upon something out of the window. Then, after a few minutes, return to the paper, and carefully, and slowly re-read the questions. Often, the problem is short-lived, and once you have taken a second look at the paper, the meaning of the questions becomes clearer, and things settle down. Choose a short, simple question to begin with, and gradually the nervousness will subside. Do not be intimidated by other candidates who may be working quite furiously around you: you cannot know whether their work is of a high quality or not. Your concern must be solely for your own performance. Of course, if you have not worked for the examination, there is little help or advice which can be offered.

If when the results are published you find that you have not passed, or not done as well as you could have hoped, do not regard this as some judgement upon you as a person. You may feel disappointed, depressed, and a sense of rejection, but try to get things into proportion, and reject all negative feelings. It may be that your preparation was not as it should have been. It may be that the subject is not really one which comes 'naturally' to you. Seek advice from those whose opinions you respect, and listen to what they have to say. Do not act hastily, and do not make decisions merely to satisfy other people. Remember that many people have built their ultimate success upon some short-term failure. We often learn more from our mistakes than from our successes.

Chapter 3

Nature and scope

In order to fully understand a subject, it is necessary to become familiar with the specialist language of that subject. It is not merely a matter of knowing the meaning of the technical terms used, and being able to repeat them. In order to be able fully to discuss the concepts which lie behind the terms, it is necessary to understand the differences in meaning.

This chapter begins the process for Cost and Management Accounting by examining the meaning of basic terms and by setting them in the context of the management function. In doing this, the chapter also gives some idea of the range of organisations within which Cost and Management Accounting can usefully be employed.

Examination questions in this area tend to be of a discussive nature, requiring essays, notes, or reports concerning:

1. The definition of terms.
2. Comparisons of concepts.
3. Discussion of the role of Cost and Management Accounting.

Experience indicates that many accounting candidates are not well prepared for this type of question: candidates' answers tend to be shallow, imprecise, and badly constructed. Most accounting examinations, even at elementary levels, demand the ability to discuss definitions and concepts; and the more advanced the examination, the more this becomes necessary. Candidates should therefore give attention to developing the skills required to perform well in this area.

ESSENTIAL PRINCIPLES

Cost and Management Accounting acts as an aid to the managers of an organisation by providing them with information needed for decision making. The management function has to do with the *five* activities of planning, organisation, co-ordination, command and control.

Planning can be divided into *long-term planning* – sometimes called *strategic planning* – and *operational planning*. Long-term planning is concerned with setting an organisation's long-term objectives, and as such it is usually the prerogative of the organisation's top management. Long-term plans usually take the form of policy statements, which act as a guide for other decisions. Operational planning is concerned with preparing detailed plans to enable the long-term objectives to be met. Operational planning tends to be the role of middle and junior management.

Once decisions have been taken at the strategic and the operational levels, resources will need to be *organised* and activities *co-ordinated* to give effect to the decisions. This needs someone to take *command* and to *control* activities to ensure that operations are furthering the organisation's overall plans.

In order to make decisions and to carry out these functions, managers will require information, *some* of it in an accounting form, *Management Accounting* is concerned with providing information to help managers to:

- formulate policies;
- plan and control the activities of the organisation;
- decide on alternative courses of action;
- disclose information to employees, and to those outside the organisation;
- safeguard assets.

All of these activities involve effective participation in management to ensure the following outcomes:

- formulation of plans to meet objectives (long term planning);
- formulation of short term operational plans (budgeting, profit planning);
- recording of actual transactions (financial accounting and cost accounting);
- corrective action to bring future actual transactions into line (financial control);
- obtaining and controlling finance (treasurership);
- reviewing and reporting on systems and operations (internal audit, management audit).

In this respect, *Management Accounting* is more introspective and more proactive than *Financial Accounting*, which covers the classification and recording of actual transactions, and endeavours to present as accurate a view as possible of the effects of these transactions over a period of time. Financial accounting has to do with the stewardship functions of a business, and because of this it deals with external considerations as required by shareholders, taxation authorities, banks, and potential creditors.

Cost Accounting is *part* of Management Accounting, and is especially concerned with establishing budgets and standard costs, and with the actual costs of operations, processes, departments, products, or services. Cost Accounting also has to do with comparing actual performance against planned performance through the examination of *variances*. Cost Accounting therefore tends to be more basic than Management Accounting, which tends to be concerned more with the interpretation of that accounting information which Cost Accounting produces. Although it is possible to distinguish Cost and Management Accounting from Financial Accounting, it is not so easy to distinguish Cost Accounting from Management Accounting, and the two terms are usually used together.

It is through an organisation's costing system that the management accountant obtains the information necessary to support the management function; just what sort of costing system is adopted by an organisation will depend upon its structure, its technology, the data it has decided to collect, and the reasons for that collection.

One of the main purposes of Cost Accounting is to control expenditure, and this requires the tracing of costs to those employees who have direct influence over them. *Cost centres* are locations, functions, or items of equipment for which costs can be gathered, and related to *cost units* for purposes of control. A *cost unit* is a quantitative unit of product or service in relation to which costs are ascertained: in the mining industry, therefore, costs may be calculated as so much per tonne, whereas a papermaker may calculate costs as so much per ream.

Expenses incurred by service departments – such as safety and welfare – have to be traced to cost centres which provide a service, rather than to productive cost centres. Because of this, they are sometimes called *service centres*.

ELEMENTS OF COST

The *cost* of a product or service is the money incurred on or attributable to it. Cost comprises *direct costs* which are those expenses which can be identified precisely as attaching to the product, and *indirect costs* which cannot easily be traced to the product. The relationship between direct costs and *indirect costs* is given by the following equations:

Direct Materials	+ Direct Labour	+ Direct Expenses	= Prime Cost
Indirect Materials	+ Indirect Labour	+ Indirect Expenses	= Overheads
Prime Cost	+ Production Overheads		= Production Cost
Production Cost	+ Sales, Distribution, and Administration Overheads		= Total Cost

All costs other than prime costs are *indirect costs*. The total of the indirect costs represents the *overhead costs*: in some American organisations, the term *burden* may be used.

PRODUCT AND PERIOD COSTS

Product cost is the cost of a finished product built up from its cost elements. *Period costs* are costs which accrue over the passage of time, and which tend to be unaffected by the level of output, over certain ranges of activity. Rent and rates are examples. These expenses must be paid as long as the business occupies the premises, irrespective of whether anything is produced or not. Alternative names for period costs are *policy costs* and *fixed overhead costs*.

USEFUL APPLIED MATERIALS

Some idea of the tasks performed by cost and management accountants can be gained by studying the advertisements in the professional journals. The advertisement shown in Fig. 3.1 refers to a *Cost and Works Accountant*. When the Chartered Institute of Management Accountants was formed in 1919, it was known as the Institute of Cost and Works Accountants – a name which emphasised its relationship to factory accounting. As can be seen from the advertisement, the name is still used. Study the duties to be performed by the appointee.

A *cost unit* is a unit of product or service in relation to which costs are ascertained. The extract shown in Fig. 3.2 is taken from the Department of Education and Science's Annual Report for 1985. It shows net recurrent expenditure per *full-time equivalent pupil/student*.

Fig. 3.1

LONDON BOROUGH OF TOWER HAMLETS
An Equal Opportunity Employer
Directorate of Housing
COST AND WORKS ACCOUNTANT

Our Direct Labour Organisation Division with a labour force of 800 men requires a Cost and Works Accountant to be responsible for all aspects of production costing.

Reporting to the Cost Control Manager you will be responsible for the following:

- Implementation and upgrading the standard costing system
- Preparation of Management Accounting Reports
- The Division's Budget
- Providing the control information services to the Operations Management

You should be a qualified CIMA with a minimum of 2 years' experience preferably in the Building Industry or Manufacturing.

The Council is decentralising its services and all offers of appointments are made on the understanding that job location, duties and responsibilities are liable to change.

Applications for the above post are invited from qualified and experienced persons. Application form and job description may be obtained from the Personnel Reception, Town Hall, Patriot Square, London E2 9LN, or telephone our answering service on 01-981 0000.

Please quote the job title and reference. Completed forms must be returned by 20th October 1986.

Applications are considered on their suitability for the post, regardless of sex, sexual orientation, religion, racial origin, marital status, disablement or age.

Source: London Borough of Tower Hamlets

Fig. 3.2
Net institutional recurrent expenditure per full-time equivalent pupil/student

	1983–84	1984–85
Non-university education (England)		
Maintained schools		
Nursery	1,215	1,290
Primary		
– all	730	760
– nursery classes	855	865
– ordinary classes	725	760
Secondary		
– all	1,015	1,085
– pupils aged 11–16	965	1,030
– pupils aged 16-plus	1,545	1,650
Special education	3,255	3,560
Post-school education		
Adult Education Centres	790	850
Polytechnics		
– all work	2,990	3,030
– advanced work	2,975	3,015
– non-advanced work	3,375	3,530
Major establishments of FE		
– all work	2,230	2,325
– advanced work	3,010	3,120
– non-advanced work	2,095	2,190
Universities (Great Britain)	4,895	n/a

Source: Department of Education and Science Annual Report 1985

RECENT EXAMINATION QUESTIONS

Discussive questions always demand that you plan your answer carefully before beginning to write. Compile a brief answer plan, listing the points which you intend to discuss. Then, go through your list, ranking the points in the order in which you intend to use them. It may be, of course, that at this stage you realise that perhaps the question is different from what you first thought, and you may abandon it for another. But how much better to discover that before you have spent valuable time on it.

Question **1** seeks to test whether you understand the relationship between different classes of cost, and requires a diagrammatic answer. Question **2** tests definitions more traditionally, and requires you to apply them. The remaining questions test whether you can set the role of Cost and Management Accounting within the management context. Question **3** is chosen for the *Tutor's Answer*.

1 Draw a diagram showing how the elements of cost, both direct and indirect, combine to give total cost of goods sold.

(20 marks)
(LCC Intermediate, Spring 1986)

2

(i) Explain the terms 'cost centre' and 'cost unit';
(ii) Suggest suitable cost units which may be used to aid control within the following organisations:
    (1) a hospital;
    (2) a road haulage business;
    (3) a hotel with 40 double rooms and 5 single rooms;
    (4) a public transport authority.

(10 marks)
(CIMA Specimen, Stage 2, 1986)

3 'If the management accountant searches for a system that will provide the "true cost" of each type of good or service produced by his firm, he is attempting the impossible.' Comment.

(5 marks)
(ACCA Level 2, June 1984)

4 Describe the role of the cost accountant in a manufacturing organisation.

(8 marks)
(ACCA Level 1, December 1984)

5 The management process centres on the key activities of planning, organisation, co-ordination, command, and control. How does the work of the cost and management accountant contribute to the management process?

(20 marks)
(ULSEB, 'A' Level, June 1984)

Fig. 3.3

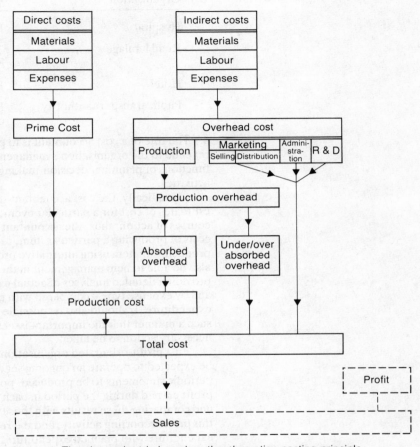

Notes: 1. The above chart is based on the absorption costing principle.
2. In the case of marginal costing, the amount of production overhead absorbed would relate to the variable element only.

2
(i)   A **cost centre** is a location, function, or items of equipment in respect of which costs may be ascertained and related to cost units for control purposes. A **cost unit** is a quantitative unit of product or service in relation to which costs are ascertained.

       Thus, a cost centre is a *specific function* such as a paint shop in a car factory, to which costs are allocated and apportioned. However, a cost unit is a *product* which is produced, or a *service* which is provided by an organisation, such as for example, the production of a car or the provision of electricity. Costs incurred in the production of each unit of product or in the provision of each unit of service are ascertained, so that costs can be controlled by management.

(ii)
Organisation	Cost unit
Hospital	Patient/day
Road haulage	Tonne/kilometre or ton/mile
Hotel	Room/day occupied
Public transport authority	Passenger/kilometre or passenger/mile

4   The role of a cost accountant is to provide data on costs and revenue to the organisation's management to help them in their functions of planning, decision-making, and the controlling of activities.

Specifically, the cost accountant should be able to provide estimates of cost for a particular event, or the costs of *alternative* courses of action: thus, the accountant should be able to show the costs of producing a particular item, or the comparative costs of producing an item using alternative processes. The accountant should also be able to help management in their controlling activities by providing detailed analyses of actual expenditures – by department, and by expense type – compared with target, or budgeted expenditure. It should also be possible to present these analyses in such a manner that the important issues can be isolated, enabling the necessary action to be taken.

In a profit-orientated organisation, the cost accountant will also be expected to operate an ongoing set of cost accounts to enable periodic statements to be produced, possibly monthly, showing the profit earned during the period in each of the organisation's activities, and comparing these results with those for previous periods. Often, this profit-reporting activity, and the regular comparison of actual expenditure with planned expenditure, will be combined in the production of a periodic set of 'operating statements'.

5   The answer here should discuss each of the five key activities, and should relate Cost and Management Accounting techniques to each one. Thus:

Planning:	budgetary control; standard costing
Organisation:	cost centres, service centres, departments
Co-ordination:	aims of organisation, policies, master budget
Command:	decision-making, pricing policies, investment appraisal
Control:	information needed: costs, revenues, profits.

3   The management accountant is concerned to provide relevant information to an organisation's management. The cost accounting system is intended to record data in such a framework that costing data can be easily extracted as required. Thus, conventionally, organisations calculate as a matter of routine a cost for each of the goods or services which they provide.

Unit cost information is frequently required, so that the management accountant will attempt to ensure that it is timely, complete, relevant, and 'true'. However, care must be taken in searching for the 'true cost', since the truth of any cost calculation can be judged only in relation to the purpose for which it is required. Thus, a cost relevant for fixing prices may not be appropriate for stock valuation, or for budgeting purposes.

The cost accountant, may, therefore, attempt to ensure that the organisation's costing system provides cost figures which are relevant to those business problems which regularly occur within that organisation. However, even here it may be necessary to compromise, since there may be no single cost figure which is entirely suitable for particular problems. It may, therefore, be useful to regard the costing system as a data bank, for which relevant cost information can be extracted as needed, rather than as a system which attempts to calculate a true cost for each of a firm's goods or services.

A cost is always related to a possible decision in a given situation. Therefore, a cost can only be described as 'true' if it is entirely relevant to that specific problem at that time. Generally, management accountants cannot be expected to provide such true information 'off the peg' for every conceivable problem. They therefore provide such information as seems relevant given the constraints within which they work: a true cost uniquely applicable to particular situations does not exist.

The following are a selection of books which cover the nature of Cost and Management Accounting, and which discuss the various elements of cost. Do try to consult two or three of the texts, because each author will deal with the topics in a different manner, and may emphasise different aspects.

Arnold and Hope, *Accounting for Management Decision*. Prentice Hall, Chs 1 and 3.
Daff, *Cost and Management Accounting*. Woodhead Faulkner, Ch. 1.
Drury, *Management and Cost Accounting*. Van Nostrand Reinhold, Ch. 1.
Harvey and Nettleton, *Management Accounting*. Mitchell Beazley, Ch. 1.
Lucey, *Costing*. D P Publications, Chs 1, 2 and 3.
Lucey, *Management Accounting*. D P Publications, Chs 1, 4, 5, and 6.
Riddle, *Stage I Cost Accounting*. Northwick, Chs 1 and 2.

Chapter 4

Material costs

GETTING STARTED

For many organisations, a large proportion of total production cost is accounted for by the cost of materials used in manufacture. Large sums of money are invested in stocks of materials and components, some of which require specialist and expensive storage facilities, either to ensure the qualities of the material, or for security.

Questions in this area tend to be very popular with many examining bodies. Calculation questions tend to concentrate upon:

1. The working of the methods FIFO, LIFO, and AVCO – on both perpetual and periodic bases.
2. The effects of each of the methods upon stock valuations, and profits.
3. The calculation of economic order quantities, and re-order levels.

Discussive questions tend to emphasise:

1. Comparisons of the different methods of valuing materials issues.
2. The selection of methods in different circumstances.
3. The functions and operation of materials and stores control procedures.
4. General description of the necessary accounting systems.

Some syllabuses emphasise stock control procedures, and methods of stocktaking more than others; it is wise to check your own particular syllabus.

ESSENTIAL PRINCIPLES

The whole purpose of stock control is to ensure that the right materials and components as required by production are in the right place at the right time, and in the right quantities; and this with the minimum investment of capital.

Typical problems for organisations are shortage of items, the holding of excessive stocks, large amounts of obsolete stock, overfull stores, and stock losses.

The particular needs of production will determine the precise nature of the stock control system used, but generally, the following characteristics will be present:

- classification of items by type, location, or use, each item having a unique code;
- proper storage facilities to safeguard quality and security; in the case of dangerous items, storage facilities may be subject to legal requirements;
- an effective stock record system to enable either regular stock checks, or a system of continuous stocktaking;
- proper accounting and costing procedures for all items of stock and stores expenses to enable full analysis and control.

STORES PROCEDURE

Detailed procedures will differ with different organisations, but common themes will be apparent. It is usually better for one person, or department, to be responsible for all purchasing: this enables the necessary expertise to be built up, and eases control over ordering. Only official orders, signed by nominated officers should be used.

The ordering sequence begins when the stores request the purchasing department to order a specified quantity of a particular item for delivery at a stated location by a stated time. The purchase department will then raise the order with the supplier, and send the stores a copy of the order.

When the items are received, they should be checked against the copy order, and inspected to ensure that they are received in good condition; breakages or spoiled items will almost certainly have to be reported to the supplier within a specified time, otherwise claims for damaged items may be affected.

Requests for items from the stores should be made in the official manner, and on the prescribed requisition, signed by a responsible member of staff; items returned to the stores in excess of requirement should also be documented in an agreed manner. In this way, a proper audit trail is provided to aid analysis and control. When items are issued, the stores must amend its records of stockholding; and this may be done on a *bin card*. A bin card is a prime entry record of stock quantity, kept by the stores on an in-out basis.

This whole routine may demand the use of commercial documents such as:

- **Advice note**   A document prepared to advise a third party in advance of the despatch of goods.
- **Credit note**   A document prepared by the seller notifying the purchasers that their account is being reduced by a stated amount because of an allowance, return of goods, or cancellation.

- **Debit note** A document prepared by the purchaser notifying the sellers that their account has been reduced by a stated amount because of an allowance, return of goods, or cancellation.
- **Delivery note** A document which accompanies goods for delivery and may act as proof of delivery, sometimes called a *consignment note* or a *carrier's note*.
- **Despatch note** A document prepared to advise a third party of actual quantity, date of despatch and method of transportation.
- **Goods received note** A document prepared by a recipient to record receipt of goods, either because an advice note has not been received, or to create a common format within the recipient's system.
- **Invoice** A document prepared by a supplier showing the description, quantities, price, and value of goods delivered, or of services performed. To the supplier it is a *sales invoice*; to the purchaser it is a *purchase invoice*.
- **Materials requisition** A document which requests and authorises the issue of materials from the stores.
- **Materials returned note** A document which records the return of unused materials to the stores.
- **Pro-forma invoice** An invoice sent to the purchaser in advance of goods, usually requesting that payment be made before the goods are despatched.
- **Purchase order** A document ordering goods or services from a supplier, specifying price, quantity, delivery dates, and terms for a purchase contract.
- **Purchase requisition** A document from a stores to a buying office requesting the purchase of goods or services.
- **Sales order** A document issued by a supplier as an acknowledgement of a purchase order, which may over-ride the buyer's purchase terms.

There are three general patterns for stores organisation:

1. Centralised buying and holding of stores;
2. Centralised purchasing of stores, but decentralised handling of materials;
3. Decentralised buying and handling of stores.

The advantages of centralised buying were dealt with above. The advantages of centralised *materials handling* are that it leads to economies in the cost of staffing and of storage space; enables expertise to be developed in material handling; improves supervision, security, and administration; enables a better laying out of stores, and makes maximum use of specialist equipment such as cranes, conveyor belts, tanks, etc.; enables stocks to be kept at a minimum; and generally improves the efficiency of stock taking and control.

The drawbacks include: increased transport costs if the stores are some distance from the user; possible delays in obtaining materials from a centralised store; increased risk that anything that disrupts the central store will affect all production, e.g. a fire in the stores.

The establishment of a number of *substores* may go some way to resolving some of these problems, whilst at the same time preserving some of the advantages of centralisation. Sometimes, the substores will operate on an *imprest system* of storekeeping: here, a level of stockholding is identified for each store and for each item of stock. At the end of the month, the storekeeper merely requisitions from the central store that amount necessary to bring the holding up to the imprest amount.

STORES CONTROL

The efficient running of any organisation demands a planned flow of materials to service the activities. If stocks are kept at too high a level, storage costs will be high, and much money will be tied up in an illiquid asset. On the other hand, if insufficient stocks are available, there is a greater risk of *stock outs*, with the consequent effect upon production.

Five main considerations apply:

- **Stock out costs** The costs of running out of stock can be very high, especially where continuous processes are concerned.
- **Stockholding costs** Keeping materials in store incurs expenses: rent and rates may be payable. Again, where specialist facilities are needed, there may be high additional expenses involved. This may be true of corrosive substances, of items that require refrigeration, or that have to be kept under pressure, as with gases.
- **Production rates** Because raw materials are for use in production, stock levels will change as the production rate varies.
- **Procurement costs** The act of placing an order costs the firm money: the salaries and wages of the clerical staff, and the overheads of the purchasing and accounts departments, for example. The fewer the number of orders placed, the lower will the procurement costs tend to be. However, reductions in procurement costs gained through bulk buying, must be offset against the additional stockholding costs.
- **Cost of finance** Money invested in stocks cannot be used for anything else. There is therefore an *opportunity cost* involved in purchasing raw materials: opportunity cost is defined as the value of a benefit sacrificed as a result of taking a particular course of action. Thus, money spent on stocks cannot be spent on new equipment. In practice, many firms equate opportunity cost with the level of external interest rates.

Stock control is essentially about balancing these various costs, some of which move in opposite directions. If orders are placed infrequently, procurement costs will be kept down, but stockholding costs may increase: if, however, stocks are kept low, stockholding costs may be reduced, but there will be an increased risk of stocking out.

Various mathematical techniques have been developed to help managers to resolve these difficulties, and some of the methods involved are quite complicated. Three of the more straightforward are identified below:

Re-order levels

The stock level at which further supplies should be ordered is given by the equation:

$$\text{Re-order level} = U \times L + M$$

where U is the usage per period t, L is the lead time expressed as a fraction of t, and M is the minimum stock level.

Re-order quantity

The *economic order quantity* shows the optimum amount to be ordered on each occasion, once the re-order level has been reached, the equation here is:

$$\text{Economic order quantity} = \sqrt{\frac{2UC}{H}}$$

where U is rate of usage in time t, C is the cost of placing an order, H is the holding cost per unit.

Pareto 80/20 distribution

Named after the economist Vilfredo Pareto, who applied the notion to the distribution of wealth in the economy. The concept has since been applied to many other issues, including that of stock control. Here, it refers to the idea that in many companies, 80 per cent of the value of stock is tied up in 20 per cent of the quantity of stock. Rigorous control of this 20 per cent is therefore likely to be more important than strict control of the remaining items. The Pareto distribution can also be depicted in graphical terms, as the answer to Question **5** illustrates (p. 40).

VALUING MATERIALS ISSUES

Where items used in production can be readily identified, then they may be issued at the price which was paid for them. However, where materials lose their separate identity, and where price changes are apparent, some conventional means must be adopted in charging materials to production. There are a number of such methods available, but the most common are *FIFO* (first in, first out) *LIFO* (last in, first out) and *AVCO* (average cost). Each of these methods may be used on a *perpetual* or *periodic* basis.

Under FIFO the earliest stock is *assumed* to be issued first: under LIFO the latest stock is *assumed* to be issued first. With AVCO, the issue price is recalculated each time there is a new receipt. With AVCO, too, certain slight inaccuracies may occur due to 'rounding off' errors.

Because each method gives a different figure for the closing stock, each will result in a different profit figure.

The *perpetual* method – whether FIFO, LIFO, or AVCO – requires the recalculation of stock values after each transaction. Conversely, the *periodic* approach ignores the timing of the transactions, and calculates the value of the issues retrospectively over the period.

LIFO and AVCO will usually give different stock values depending upon whether perpetual or periodic methods are used. FIFO will give the same stock figure under both perpetual and periodic methods.

FIFO, LIFO, AND AVCO COMPARED

None of the methods can be said to be 'right' or in any way 'better' than the others. FIFO will tend to give a more realistic measure for closing stock than does LIFO, since FIFO values stock at current prices; but FIFO will give a less realistic figure for materials issued, since it is using outdated prices here.

Conversely, LIFO will give an unrealistic figure for closing stock, but an up-to-date valuation for materials used.

AVCO avoids the extremes of both of the other two methods, but it uses values for issues that are not actual prices as paid; and because it demands slightly more complex calculations, the method may be more prone to errors.

THE PHYSICAL ISSUES OF STOCK

There really is no inherent connection between the accounting system a company may use, and the way in which stocks are *actually* issued. Thus, a company may account for its materials issues on a FIFO basis, and yet for ease of operation, may elect to issue the latest items first; this may be true of ores taken from a stocking ground. Similarly, a jam making factory may use the older fruit first – because it is perishable – and yet account for it on a LIFO basis.

The need for some accounting convention arises solely because of price changes: were prices to remain constant, there would be no need of such systems as FIFO, LIFO, or AVCO.

SSAP 9

The Statement of Standard Accounting Practice (SSAP) 9 has to do with the valuation of stocks and work-in-progress. In an appendix, the SSAP rejects LIFO as a method, but says nothing about FIFO or AVCO. LIFO is not commonly used in the UK, but it is found in the USA and is used by UK subsidiaries of American companies. Note, however, that the SSAP refers to the valuation of stocks in published accounts: companies are free to use whatever method they wish for internal management purposes.

STOCKTAKING

Periodic stocktaking occurs when every so often a complete physical check is done to count every item of stock, and to compare the results with the stock records. Such an operation is usually mounted over a holiday, or a weekend, when the productive departments are not demanding items from the stores. This actual count is known as the taking of a *physical inventory*.

For large organisations, such a periodic stock check can be a major operation, and can disrupt normal routines. For this reason, many companies operate a system of perpetual stock checking – sometimes called the *perpetual inventory* method. Here, each time an item is removed from the stores, the storeman checks the physical quantities against those entered on the bin card, or similar record, and discrepancies are reported as they are discovered, instead of waiting until a periodic check.

USEFUL APPLIED MATERIALS

Increasingly, costing records are being kept, not in ledgers or on cards, but on micro computers. The task of recording the movement of stock items, and the changes in stock levels and valuations is ideally suited to computer operations, since the movement of stock makes necessary a continual amendment of the records.

Fig. 4.1 Use of a spreadsheet file

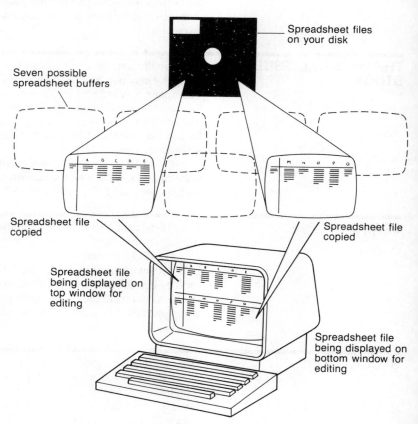

Spreadsheet files on your disk

Seven possible spreadsheet buffers

Spreadsheet file copied

Spreadsheet file copied

Spreadsheet file being displayed on top window for editing

Spreadsheet file being displayed on bottom window for editing

As with many costing applications, the use of computerised *spreadsheets* eases the recording activity. Spreadsheets are simply a matrix of lines and columns upon which data can be entered and calculations performed. By using electronic spreadsheets, time-consuming calculations can be given over to the computer, so that changes in, say, stock levels and stock valuations can be recorded quite literally at the touch of a button.

RECENT EXAMINATION QUESTIONS

Questions **1**, **2**, **3**, **5**, and **6** are discussive questions testing an understanding of various aspects of materials control, and stock handling procedures. Question **4** is a calculation question involving AVCO perpetual, and FIFO, LIFO, and AVCO periodic; as with many questions at intermediate levels, you are asked to explain your answers. Question **7** is a lengthy question looking at cost behaviour, and raw materials costs and control; because it is a lengthy question touching upon a number of important issues, Question **7** is the one chosen for the *Tutor's Answer*.

1 Describe the essential requirements of an effective stock control system.

(17 marks)
(ACCA Level 1, June 1985)

2 Describe and discuss the relative merits of the various methods that may be used for pricing the issue of raw materials to production.

(17 marks)
(ACCA Level 1, June 1986)

3
(i) Explain the factors to be considered when devising stock control procedures.
(ii) What techniques are available to help firms balance competing costs in relation to stockholding?

(20 marks)
(ULSEB, 'A' Level, January 1987)

4 A company uses the AVCO (average cost) perpetual inventory method of charging items to production. Details of receipts and issues for the six months to 31 December 1985 were:

	Receipts	*Issues*	
16 July	10 @ £16	19 July	6
2 August	14 @ £17	26 July	8
7 September	26 @ £17.50	10 August	12
29 September	18 @ £18	14 September	24
4 November	12 @ £18	26 October	15
15 December	15 @ £18.40	21 November	8

Opening stock at 1 July 1985 comprised 8 items with a total value of £124.

(a) What would be the value of closing stock using the AVCO perpetual inventory method?

(12 marks)

(b) Using the periodic inventory method, calculate the value of closing stock using:
    (i)   AVCO (average cost)
    (ii) FIFO (first in, first out)
    (iii) LIFO (last in, first out)

(13 marks)

(c) Explain briefly why you obtain a different answer in (b)(i) from (a) above.

(5 marks)

(ULSEB, 'A' Level, January 1986)

5

(a) (i)   Explain the term 'materials control' indicating the scope of its coverage within a manufacturing business;
    (ii) Differentiate between 'stock control' and 'storekeeping';
    (iii) Explain the term 'Pareto 80/20 distribution'.

(10 marks)

(b) Demonstrate your understanding of (a)(iii) above by:
    (i) Classifying for stock purposes, the items shown below;
    (ii) Drawing a graph that will enable management to understand the significance of your classification in (b)(i).

Table 4.1

Stock item reference no.	Annual usage (units)	Cost/unit (£)
7212	1,200	62.5
7213	800	150.0
7214	1,400	15.0
7215	2,000	11.4
7216	2,600	12.0
7217	5,000	3.2
7218	5,000	1.6
7219	2,000	3.0

(15 marks)

(CIMA Foundation Stage, November 1984)

6 You have been given full responsibility for the stocktaking of your company's inventory and its subsequent valuation. There are approximately 4,000 different categories of stock ranging from small components to finished products.

(a) Detail the factors required in order to achieve an efficient stocktake and inventory valuation.

(8 marks)

(b) How would you recognise and deal with obsolescent stock and
slow moving stock?

(7 marks)

(c) What is a perpetual inventory system? What benefits would
accrue from its installation?

(7 marks)

(AAT Level 3, June 1984)

7 A company is reviewing the purchasing policy for one of its raw
materials as a result of a reduction in production requirement. The
material, which is used evenly throughout the year, is used in only
one of the company's products, the production of which is currently
12,000 units per annum. Each finished unit of the product contains
0.4 kilograms of the material: 20 per cent of the material is lost in
the production process. Purchases can be made in multiples of 500
kilograms, with a minimum purchase order quantity of 1,000
kilograms.

The cost of the raw material depends upon the purchase order
quantity as follows:

Order quantity (kg)	Cost per kg (£)
1,000	1.00
1,500	0.98
2,000	0.965
2,500	0.95
3,000 and above	0.94

Costs of placing and handling each order are £90, of which £40 is an
apportionment of costs which are not expected to be affected in the
short term by the number of orders placed. Annual holding costs of
stock are £0.90 per unit of average stock, of which only £0.40 is
expected to be affected in the short term by the amount of stock
held. The lead time for the raw material is one month, and a safety
stock of 250 kilograms is required.

(a) Explain, and illustrate from the situation described above the
meaning of the terms 'variable', 'semi variable', and 'fixed'
costs.

(8 marks)

(b) Calculate the annual cost of pursuing alternative purchase order
policies and thus advise the company regarding the purchase
order quantity for the material that will minimise the cost.

(14 marks)

(ACCA Level 1, December 1985)

1 This question is designed to test knowledge of the systems, information and control routines necessary for effective material stock control. The essential requirements of an effective system comprise:

- Clear delegation of responsibility – who should do what?
- Adequate, and up-to-date stock records for each item; use of codes to classify each item.
- Re-order levels, re-order quantities, minimum and maximum stock levels for each item.
- Regular comparison of target stock levels with actual stock levels; reviewing of targets in the light of the organisation's likely change in requirements.
- Orders from the stores to the purchasing office, issues from the stores to production, and any items returned to the stores should be accompanied by the official documentation, properly signed by the authorised officer.
- All goods received from suppliers should be physically checked, and compared to the documentation before being taken into the stores.
- Perpetual stock records should be checked regularly, either by a system of continuous stocktaking, or by a periodic and complete physical stocktake.
- Regular reports to management on the quantity and value of stocks held; such reports will often group similar items of stock together for ease of analysis.
- Application of the 80/20 (Pareto) rule, and its implications.
- Restricted access to stores to maintain security.
- Well planned physical layout of stores; care taken to keep stores areas tidy.

2 A straightforward, discussive question, requiring comparisons to be made amongst AVCO, FIFO, and LIFO. Do be sure to offer a balanced answer: each of the methods has good qualities, depending upon the situation. Explain.

3

(i) You should examine the effect of centralised and decentralised stockholding upon stores control procedures; mention, too, the imprest system of stockholding. The question also demands an explanation of the five considerations: stock out costs; stockholding costs; production rates; procurement costs; and the cost of finance. You should state which of the influences are likely to move in opposition, and why.

(ii) The techniques to be discussed include the economic order quantity, the re-order level, and the Pareto 80/20 distribution. You should explain the workings of each thoroughly, providing a simple numerical example to illustrate your comments.

4

(a) The following answer (Table 4.2) is based upon weighted averages, which are to be preferred when using the AVCO method. Note that there may be slight differences in answers due to the rounding-off errors: in examinations, marks would be awarded provided your answer was plus/minus £2 of the total stock figures given. (Note, too, how the layout of the information lends itself to spreadsheet applications.)

Table 4.2

	Receipts			Issues			Stocks		
	No.	(£)	(£)	No.	(£)	(£)	No.	(£)	(£)
1 July (opening stock)							8	15.50	124.00
16 July	10	16.0	160				18	15.78	284.00
19 July				6	15.78	94.68	12	15.78	189.32
26 July				8	15.78	126.24	4	15.78	63.08
2 August	14	17.0	238				18	16.73	301.08
10 August				12	16.73	200.76	6	16.73	100.32
7 September	26	17.5	455				32	17.35	555.32
14 September				24	17.35	416.40	8	17.35	138.92
29 September	18	18.0	324				26	17.80	462.92
26 October				15	17.80	267.00	11	17.80	195.92
4 November	12	18.0	216				23	17.91	411.92
21 November				8	17.91	143.28	15	17.91	268.64
15 December	15	18.4	276				30	18.16	544.64

(b) (i) *AVCO periodic*: Value of opening stock plus purchases = £1,793.

Number of items = 103. The average cost therefore = £1,793 ÷ 103 = £17.41.

The number of items in stock at 30 December = 30: the stock valuation thus is £17.41 × 30 = £522.30.

(ii) *FIFO periodic*: (15 × £18.4) + (12 × £18) + (3 × £18) = £546

(iii) *LIFO periodic*: (8 × £15.5) + (10 × £16) + (12 × £17) = £488

(c) In the periodic method, all items of stock are valued at the average price of £17.41. In the perpetual method, a moving average is calculated after each stock movement.

5

(a) (i) *Materials control*: planning, ordering, receiving, storing, issuing, and control of materials, plus control of stocks of raw materials, work-in-progress, and finished goods.

(ii) *Stock control*: regulating stock levels of raw materials, work-in-progress, and finished goods re quantity, cost, and lead time. *Storekeeping* includes requisitioning, receiving supplies, storing, recording, issuing materials, and maintaining effective stock levels.

(b) (i)

Table 4.3

Stock items	Percentage of quantity			Price	Percentage of value		
Ref. No.	Units	%	%	(£)	%	%	(£)
Class A							
7212	1,200	6.0	—	62.5	25.0	—	75,000
7213	800	4.0	10	150.0	40.0	65	120,000
Class B							
7214	1,400	7.0	—	15.0	7.0	—	21,000
7215	2,000	10.0	—	11.4	7.6	—	22,800
7216	2,600	13.0	30	12.0	10.4	25	31,200
Class C							
7217	5,000	25.0	—	3.2	5.3	—	16,000
7218	5,000	25.0	—	1.6	2.7	—	8,000
7219	2,000	10.0	60	3.0	2.0	10	6,000
	20,000	100.0			100.0		300,000

(ii) *Pareto Curve*:

Fig. 4.2

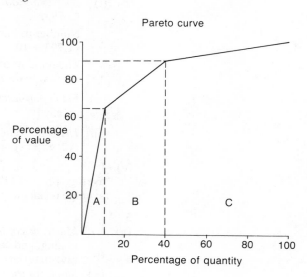

Pareto curve

A High value stock
B Medium value stock
C Low value stock

(iii) *Pareto distribution*: 80 per cent of value of stock represented by 20 per cent of quantity of stock.

6

(a) Prepare and issue stocktaking instructions well before due date, detailing specific personnel required to count particular items; agree cut-off time, and ensure no stock movements until stocktake completed. Issue pre-printed stock sheets to personnel, detailing what stock they should count, and location. Inform accounts staff of cut-off, and give instructions re accruals affecting purchases and sales. Ensure system used is comparable with that used in the past, and in accordance with SSAP 9. Senior managers to carry out sample checks on physical stocktake, and valuations; ensure auditors receive fullest co-operation.

(b) Obsolescence means reduction in value due to new invention or design modification. Stock which has had no receipts or issues over the past 12 months may not be necessary to current production – check. If no longer usable, then write off, and remove from stores in accordance with SSAP 9.

Slow moving stocks are those which show small adjustments relative to overall holding; may arise because of obsolescence or overstocking; enquire as to likely future demand; excess stock, treat as obsolescent.

(c) Perpetual inventory system maintains a continuous record of receipts, issues, and balances for every item of stock; bin cards, production control records, and stores ledger accounts are examples.

Benefits include: stores staff more responsible for reconciling physical stocks with recorded stocks; eases stores audit, since stock may be counted at frequent intervals; likely to lead to improved stock control through the fixing of maximum, minimum, and re-order levels; less likely to run out of stock, or to overstock.

A TUTOR'S ANSWER

7 This question is designed to test an understanding of cost behaviour, and the relevance of information for decision-making. The question also tests the area of raw material cost, planning and control. It is likely to be the most involved question on this topic that you meet at intermediate levels. It does, however, cover a number of important points, and has therefore been included here.

(a) Variable costs change in response to changes in activity; fixed costs do not change with different activity levels. This may be true over short ranges of output, but in the long term, all costs are variable.

In the question, if the company continues to buy material in lots of 1,000 kilograms, then the cost per unit remains the same – unit costs are fixed – and total material costs vary in proportion to the amount of product produced and sold.

However, if the level of productive activity influences the purchase order quantity, and this in turn affects the cost per unit, then materials may be regarded as a semi-variable cost. Whether they are so regarded will depend upon the range of activity being considered, the frequency of changes in purchasing policy in response to changes in activity, and the extent of the variation from proportionate variability over the range of activity being considered. Generally, we assume that the relationship is linear, i.e. that the relationship can be depicted by a straight line on a graph.

In the question, £40 of the costs of placing and handling the orders are fixed in the short term – possibly the staffing costs. Also, with holding costs, some may be fixed in the short term (such as space costs), but may in the long term be influenced by the level of production.

(b) *Annual usage of material*:

$$= 12{,}000 \text{ units } \times (0.4 \text{ kg} \div 0.8 \text{ yield})$$
$$= 6{,}000 \text{ kg}$$

Table 4.4 Annual costs of different order quantities

Order quantity (kg)	Purchase cost (£)		Placing and handling costs (£)		Holding cost (£)		Total (£)	
	Short term	Long term	Short term	Long term	Short term	Long term	Short term	Long term
1,000	6,000	6,000	300	540	300	675	6,600	7,215
1,500	5,880	5,880	200	360	400	900	6,480	7,140
2,000	5,790	5,790	150	270	500	1,125	6,440	7,185
2,500	5,700	5,700	120	216	600	1,350	6,420	7,266
3,000	5,640	5,640	100	180	700	1,575	6,440	7,395
3,500	5,640	5,640	86	154	800	1,800	6,526	7,594

Table 4.4 shows order quantities in 500 kg lots from the minimum possible of 1,000 kg up to 3,500 kg: since beyond this level no further discounts are available, it is not necessary to consider quantities above this level.

Purchase cost is based on an annual requirement of 6,000 kg as calculated and uses the information given in the question; thus, the purchase cost of 6,000 kg in 1,500 lots is 6,000 × £0.98 = £5,880; the cost of 6,000 kg in 2,500 lots is 6,000 × 0.95 = £5,700.

Placing and handling costs in the short term depend upon the variable cost of each order £50, and the number of orders placed (annual requirement ÷ order quantity). Thus, 6,000 ÷ 1,500 = 4 orders: at £50 per order, total placing and handling costs are 4 × £50 = £200. If the company's requirements are satisfied with 3 orders of 2,000 kilos each, then the costs are 3 × £50 = £150.

In the long term, all costs are variable, and thus the full £90 per order has to be borne: if the firm's needs are satisfied with six orders, each of 1,000, the long-term placing costs are 6 × £90 = £540; if two orders, each of 3,000 kg are placed, the long-term cost is 2 × £90 = £180.

Holding costs in the short term depend upon the variable cost per unit in stock of £0.40 and the average stock held. Average stock depends upon the level of safety stock, and the size of the order placed. Average stock is calculated as:

Safety stock + ½ Purchase quantity

Assume that the purchase quantity is 2,000 kg, the formula will give an average stock of:

250   +   ½(2,000)
=   1,250
1,250   ×   £0.40
=   £500

Similarly, with a purchase quantity of 3,000 kg, the average stock will be

250 + ½(3,000) = 250 + 1,500 = 1,750 : 1,750 × £0.40
= £700.

In the long term it is possible that costs per unit of stock of £0.90 are incurred as a result of increases in stock: thus, the average stock figure has to be multiplied by £0.90, rather than £0.40. This gives the long-term cost at orders of 2,000 kg as 1,250 × £0.90 = £1,125; and with orders of 3,000 kg of 1,750 × £0.90 = £1,575.

The total cost of short term and long term is achieved by adding the purchase cost plus the placing and handling costs plus the holding costs. Thus, at orders of 1,500 kg, the total cost is:

£5,880 + £200 + £400 = £6,480 short term
and £5,880 + £360 + £900 = £7,140 long term

Assuming that the company wishes to minimise the cost of materials in the short term, the optimum purchase order quantity is 2,500 kg; it is at this point that the total costs are at a minimum of £6,420. However, in the long term, the optimum quantity is 1,500 kg, since this gives the minimum long-term cost of £7,140. Much depends, of course upon the validity of the costings used.

A STEP FURTHER

The following texts cover the area of materials issues. For a full discussion of SSAP 9 see Black, *Accounting Standards*, Longman, Ch. 7.

Daff, *Cost and Management Accounting*. Woodhead Faulkner, Ch. 2.
Drury, *Management and Cost Accounting*. Van Nostrand Reinhold, Ch. 3.
Lucey, *Costing*. D P Publications, Chs 4, 5, and 6.
Lucey, *Management Accounting*. D P Publications, Ch. 13.
Norkett, *Management Accounting*. Pitman, Ch. 5.
Riddle, *Stage I Cost Accounting*. Northwick, Ch. 3.

Chapter 5

Labour costs

GETTING STARTED

Cost control has to do with the efficient use of resources. One of the largest items of *regular* expenditure for many organisations is the money it pays out on salaries, wages, bonuses and fringe benefits. The control of labour costs, therefore, is of major importance to many organisations.

As with accounting for material costs, so with labour costs, examination questions tend to test not only an ability to perform cost calculations, but also an awareness of those systems and principles which underly the accounting methods.

Discussive questions tend to test an understanding of:

1. The purposes of a wages system.
2. The accounting system necessary to record labour costs.
3. The different wages systems available under time rate, and piece rate methods.

Computational questions seek to test an ability to calculate wages costs under the different systems.

Some syllabuses require a more detailed knowledge of wages and bonus systems than do others: you should check the syllabus for the examination which you intend to take.

ESSENTIAL PRINCIPLES

Salaries tend to be paid <u>monthly</u> to <u>managers</u> and <u>administrative</u> personnel who are <u>not directly</u> involved in the productive processes. Payment is due irrespective of the level of output in the short term; and since salaries tend to be paid to someone for holding a responsible office, rather than for work done, the amount paid may be independent of <u>the hours worked</u> by the recipient.

In contrast, *wages* tend to be paid to those people who are primarily involved with <u>repetitive</u> and <u>manual activities</u>. Wages tend to be paid <u>weekly</u>, and the amount is usually governed either by the number of <u>hours worked</u> by the employee, or by the amount of <u>work done</u>.

Where wages are based upon the number of hours actually worked, <u>time-keeping</u> and its recording becomes extremely important. In the past, various methods have been used for recording workers' factory times, but by far the most common today are systems based upon clock cards. (See *Useful Applied Materials* section below.)

Each week, every employee is issued with a clock card which is kept near the department's time clock. By inserting the card into the clock upon arrival for and departure from work, each worker's factory time is automatically recorded. The clocks reset themselves each day, and some will stamp the cards in red to identify late working, or overtime. At the end of the working week, the wages office collects the cards, and uses them as a basis for calculating each employee's wages.

Whilst clock cards record employees' arrival at, and departure from, work, they do not indicate what employees were *doing* whilst at work. This may not be too important in some process industries, where the content of the working day is governed by the needs of the process: but in other industries it is vitally important to have information of what people are doing whilst at work.

In some organisations, the workers are required to keep daily or weekly *time-sheets* upon which they record the time spent on particular activities – or on particular jobs – waiting time, and other non-working time. These sheets can then be used by the cost office to calculate the cost of particular jobs, and to monitor and to control employees' activities.

Other organisations may use *job cards* (*job sheets* or *job tickets*) upon which employees enter the time they spent upon particular jobs. With such systems, idle or unallocated time must also be recorded, together with a note of the reasons for, and the duration of, such periods. An individual employee's activities during a shift can then be ascertained from the job cards and the idle time cards.

Where jobs are repetitive, firms may operate a *piece rate system*, whereby employees are paid an amount based upon the number of items they produce. Under such systems, *piece-work tickets* may be used to record work done on each item, or each batch. Alternatively, a *coupon* system may be operated, where each batch of work is accompanied by a booklet, from which employees detach a coupon when the work is completed by them. At the end of the shift, the amount of work done – and hence, the pay earned – is shown by the number of coupons held by each employee.

WAGES SYSTEMS

Wages systems operate to reward employees for work done, to act as an incentive towards greater output, to reduce overheads, to encourage efficiency, and to reduce labour turnover.

Often, *minimum wage rates* will be established by national agreements over which individual companies may have little control. Such agreements, however, may be subject to local interpretation in the light of local conditions. It is good management practice to ensure that each member of the work force understands the wages system in operation within an organisation.

Time rates are based upon the number of hours worked. These basic rates may be subject to additional premiums for overtime working. It is not uncommon for overtime hours to be paid at 'time-and-a-quarter' or 'time-and-a-half', i.e. 125 per cent or 150 per cent of the basic rate. Hours worked on Sundays may attract payment at 'double time' – 200 per cent of basic rates; and particular holidays, such as Christmas day, may attract 'treble time' – 300 per cent of basic rates.

Wages systems based upon *flat* time rates operate successfully in many industries; they are easy to understand, employees' pay is easy to calculate, and many workers like the certainty of a guaranteed amount each week. For workers such as cleaners, catering staff, and security personnel, the method is satisfactory. Flat time rate systems may also be suitable for personnel concerned more with quality than with the quantity of output: laboratory technicians, work study assistants, etc. Flat rate systems do not, however, offer any incentive to increased output.

High day rates attempt to reduce this disadvantage, by offering employees an increased hourly rate for an increased level of output. Standards of quality and of production are established by the management, so that particular tasks should be completed within set times. Special consideration is given to quality maintenance, so that increased output is not gained at the expense of reduced quality.

This approach can be carried a stage further in *measured day work* where the firm pays an agreed hourly rate in return for an increased, and specified, level of performance.

All forms of time-work are based upon the relationship between the hours worked and the hourly rate of pay. *Payment by results* schemes relate wages to output, such that any increase in output benefits the worker, whilst any diminution in output causes wages to fall. Under time rate systems, the employer tends to gain from increased activity, and to lose when output falls.

In any payment by results scheme, attention must be paid to quality, since in a drive to improve quantity, the quality of output can fall: most piece-rate schemes penalise poor quality output.

Piece rate schemes – where employees are paid so much per piece – are ideally suited to simple, repetitive tasks, and where the quality of output is determined more by the raw material and by the machines, than the operators' skill.

Do bear in mind also that no matter what the level of incentive offered, workers within that scheme will set their own acceptable level of performance based upon their financial needs, and upon their ability and willingness to work at particular levels of activity.

Straight piece work pays a specified rate for each item or batch produced. It is usual for newly appointed employees to begin to be paid on time rates until they reach a minimum standard.

Premium bonus schemes work on yet a different principle: the bonus is paid based upon the time saved in doing a job when compared to the set time for that job. The schemes make use of standard times for each task, such standards being fixed using work study techniques, past records, etc.

Three such schemes are sometimes included in examinations:

Scheme	Employees' pay
Halsey	50% of time saved
Halsey–Weir	30% of time saved
Rowan	proportion of time saved

The Halsey and Rowan schemes are named after the men who introduced them during the mid/late nineteenth century: Frederick Halsey in the USA, and James Rowan in Scotland. The Weir scheme is a variant of the Halsey method, and is so called after the name of the company wherein it was first introduced.

When illustrating the workings of these schemes, take care to calculate the worker's *hourly rate* based upon the flat rate plus the bonus. By using this approach, you can easily explain how the scheme favours the more efficient worker over, say, an eight-hour shift.

Note, too, that for initial improvements in efficiency, the Rowan scheme will generally tend to offer greater bonuses, thereafter the Halsey scheme is more favourable to the workers.

Any payment-by-results scheme must disadvantage those people who are undergoing training, and have yet to reach normal standards of output. In many firms such people receive a flat hourly rate until their performance improves sufficiently for them to go onto the bonus schemes; trainees may also be trained in a separate part of the factory to ease them into normal routines and pressures.

However, there does exist a payments scheme designed specifically for trainees. The *Barth scheme* provides for payment which is proportionately less than the actual output would otherwise earn. The scheme, which is named after its nineteenth century American creator – Carl Barth – is based on the formula:

$$\text{Earnings} = \text{Hourly rate} \times \sqrt{\begin{array}{c}\text{Standard time} \\ \text{allowed for} \\ \text{the job}\end{array} \times \begin{array}{c}\text{Time taken} \\ \text{for the} \\ \text{job}\end{array}}$$

Collective bonus schemes are based upon the output, not of individual workers, but of a team. The team may comprise all the workers in a particular shift, or department; or it may comprise all the employees in one of a company's factories.

The advantages of group schemes are that they are often easier to administer than are individual schemes; workers who are only indirectly connected with production can be included; and working arrangements within the teams can be made flexible. The drawbacks are that workers who wish to work faster than the team norm may be penalised; inefficient workers may be 'carried' by other members; and it may prove difficult to negotiate just what level of bonus shall be paid.

Various forms of such schemes exist, although few examination boards require knowledge of specific schemes: it is usually sufficient to know the general features common to all of them.

Profit sharing schemes are an effort to cultivate a feeling of commitment to the company, by giving employees a financial interest in the organisation's overall performance. Under such schemes, employees who have completed a minimum length of service qualify for an agreed share of the profits once preference shareholders have been paid, and a fixed dividend has been paid to the ordinary shareholders. If there is insufficient monies left to make these payments, then no bonus is paid.

One disadvantage of these schemes is that the profits cannot be declared until the final accounts have been properly audited, and this may be some months after the end of the company's financial year. The schemes are, however, aimed at encouraging a long-term commitment to the organisation by reducing labour turnover.

A variant of profit sharing schemes arises where a company issues non-voting shares to long serving employees. Such shares usually carry a specified maximum amount of dividend and can only be resold to trustees of the firm's profit sharing fund. By providing a long-term stake in the company's activities, such schemes go a long way towards encouraging a stable work force.

USEFUL APPLIED MATERIALS

Where time rates are used, it is important to record the hours actually spent at work, or on particular jobs. This is often done by means of *clock cards*. Fig. 5.1 is an example of a time recorder, showing a clock card inserted.

Fig. 5.1

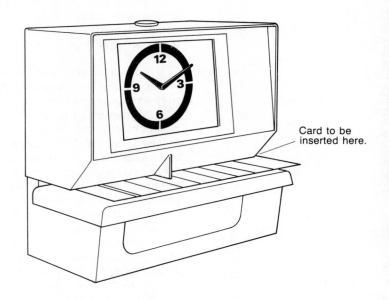

Card to be
inserted here.

1   A manufacturer, who is about to set up in business, is considering
either a day rate or a piece rate system of paying employees.

What factors should be considered before a decision is made?

(20 marks)

(ULSEB, GCE 'A' Level, January, 1985)

2   A metal component is machined in four successive operations,
particulars of which are set out below. (The times per unit include
relaxation allowances.)

Operation number	Time per unit	Grade of operator
1	30 minutes	Skilled
2	20 minutes	Skilled
3	15 minutes	Semi-skilled
4	10 minutes	Semi-skilled

Adequate machine capacity is available to meet the budgeted output
of 480 components per week. Each machine requires one operator.
The factory works a 40-hour week. Hourly wage rates for skilled and
semi-skilled operators respectively are £3.00 and £2.40.

Prepare a columnar statement showing (i) for each operation, and (ii) in total:

(a) the number of operators required (10 marks)
(b) the total labour cost per week (6 marks)
(c) the labour cost per component (4 marks)

(LCC Intermediate, Spring, 1986)

3 A small company classifies all its production overhead of £2,400 per week as fixed. The company currently produces 150 components per week on a sub-contracting basis and has been asked by its major customer to increase its output. Management is reluctant to operate for more than the normal 40 hours each week, but in an attempt to meet its customer's wishes decides to offer an incentive scheme to its four direct operators whose current rates of pay are as follows:

	Hourly rate (£)	Revised hourly rate (£)
G. Ahmed	3.00	1.50
A. Brown	3.00	1.50
D. Choudery	4.00	2.50
G. Spencer (working foreman)	5.00	3.50

With the agreement of the employees, who are not members of a trade union, their basic hourly rates are to be reduced for a trial period of four weeks to those shown above but with *each* of them being given a bonus of £0.60 for every unit produced.

After the first week of the trial period, production was 180 units. The production manager studied the results and believed the introduction of the bonus was too costly, because the increase of 20 per cent in production had increased labour costs by 32 per cent. He is considering recommending changes to the newly-introduced scheme.

(a) (i) Calculate how the increase in labour cost of 32% was derived;
    (ii) Comment on whether the production manager was correct in assuming that the bonus scheme was too costly, showing your supporting calculations.

(12 marks)

(b) List eight of the general principles which should be borne in mind when an incentive scheme for direct labour personnel is being considered.

(8 marks)

(CIMA Foundation Stage, November, 1984)

4 How can the cost accountant help to control labour costs in an organisation? What are the problems that he is likely to face in controlling labour costs?

(17 marks)

(ACCA Level 1, December, 1985)

OUTLINE ANSWERS

Question **1** tests a general understanding of different wages systems, and of the issues involved in their introduction. Question **2** is a straightforward computational question, testing an ability to perform calculations and to present the results in columnar form. Question **3** is also a computational question, but it demands an ability to interpret the results; the question also tests an understanding of incentive schemes generally. Question **4** is aimed at testing an awareness of cost accounting's role in the control of labour costs, and this is the question chosen for the *Tutor's Answer*.

1 You should compare and contrast the features of each of the main types of wages system.

Day rate:	Simple to operate and to understand; gives steady earnings each week; relevancy where care, accuracy and quality are important.
BUT:	Carries no incentive for workers to increase output.
Piece rate:	Encourages employees towards greater output, and thus meets disadvantage of time rate.
BUT:	May encourage production at the expense of quality; employees may themselves set a ceiling upon desired earnings, and therefore upon output – thus negating the incentive.

The new employer would need to look at custom and practice within the particular industry locally.

Your answer should also contain short numerical examples to illustrate the two wages systems, and should identify those occupations in which they may be found.

2

Operation	Units/ hour	Total hours	Total operatives	Cost/ unit (£)	Total cost (£)
1	2	240	6	1.5	720
2	3	160	4	1.0	480
3	4	120	3	0.6	288
4	6	80	2	0.4	192
				3.5	1,680

Operation 1 takes 30 minutes to perform: thus, 2 units can be produced each hour. If the company can manufacture 480 units per week, then the total time to manufacture this quantity is $480 \div 2 = 240$ hours. The company works a 40-hour week; the number of operatives needed to complete 240 hours is $240 \div 40 = 6$ operatives.

52

In process 1 skilled labour is used at £3.00 per hour. Since the weekly output demands 240 hours, the total cost of Operation 1 is 240 × £3.00 = £720. The weekly output of 480 units cost £720 to produce; the unit labour cost, therefore, is £720 ÷ 480 = £1.5.

The calculations for each of the other processes is as for process 1.

When the calculations have been completed for all four processes, the total cost of £1,680 is arrived at, to give a total unit cost of £1,680 ÷ 480 = £3.50.

3

(a)   (i)

Increase in Labour Cost

		(£)	(£)
			600
Current wages	40 hours @ £15		
Proposed wages	40 hours @ £9	360	
	180 units @ £2.40	432	
			792

Increase in cost $\dfrac{(£792 - £600)}{£600} \times 100 = 32\%$

Current wages are the total of the current rates: £3.00 + £3.00 + £4.00 + £5.00 = £15. The company works a 40-hour week. The *proposed wages* are the total of the revised rates: £1.50 + £1.50 + £2.50 + £3.50 = £9.00. Each of the four workers is to receive a bonus of £0.60 for every unit produced: the total bonus per unit, therefore, is 4 × £0.60 = £2.40.

(a)   (ii)

	Wages (£)	Overhead (£)	Total (£)	Output (units)	Cost/Unit (£)
Pre-bonus	600	2,400	3,000	150	20.00
Post-bonus	792	2,400	3,192	180	17.73

The cost per unit is the total cost divided by the output: thus, £3,000 ÷ 150 = £20.00; £3,192 ÷ 180 = £17.73.

The overhead of £2,400 is fixed, so that the greater the production, the smaller is the amount of overhead carried by each unit. In this example, the overhead rate per unit has reduced total unit cost by *more* than the increased cost of labour:

	Unit Cost (£)		
	Overhead	Labour	Total
Pre-bonus	16.00	4.00	20.00
Post-bonus	13.33	4.40	17.73

The production manager is therefore incorrect in assuming that the bonus scheme was too costly.

(b) The following principles should be considered:
  • full consultation and involvement at an early stage by management, and employees' representatives;
  • ensure that the proposed scheme is fully understood by all concerned;
  • establish a guaranteed minimum wage;
  • ensure that there is sufficient work available, so that employees do not lose bonus because they are waiting for work;
  • there should be sufficient motivation in the scheme to act as an incentive;
  • the scheme must be seen as being fair to all concerned;
  • the scheme must be acceptable to, and accepted by any trades union involved;
  • it may be desirable to operate a trial period so that employees do not feel prematurely committed.

A TUTOR'S ANSWER

4 Direct responsibility for controlling labour is beyond the scope of the cost accountant; but the provision of information to enable the *labour cost* to be controlled is very much the cost accountant's area.

(a) A cost accountant can seek to exert control by identifying labour costs with the work achieved. This demands both the establishment of an accounting system which can allocate labour costs to work done, *and* a meaningful measure of work achieved.

Timekeeping records will determine how labour hours are spent, so that a proper distribution can be made in the cost records. Very often, timesheets will be kept by the workers themselves of the time spent on different types of work, or on different jobs. Timesheets may be kept for a day, or for a week. Other records of labour activity may take the form of job tickets, or piece work tickets.

Detailed time-keeping is more likely to help in cost control where employees are directly engaged upon the production of saleable products, rather than upon internally used services. Where a direct worker's time cannot be allocated directly to a cost unit, some other way must be found to account for it. All indirect work by a direct worker, along with idle time, should be recorded and presented to management in such a way as will show clearly the size of, and the reasons for, such working.

Where detailed time-keeping is unlikely to be useful, the cost accountant can ensure that information for cost control is provided by establishing cost centres, and by allocating costs to those centres.

(b) The problems involved with controlling labour costs centre around the issue of comparing actual performance with expected performance. To do this successfully, it is necessary to:
- identify a required relationship between labour inputs and the services or products resulting, and
- identify useful and meaningful variances comparing actual with planned performance.

The easier it is to provide measures of work done, the greater the likelihood that performance standards can be established. For this reason, standards for repetitive operations tend to be the more easily established. Standards for non-repetitive activities can be very difficult; thus, setting standards for safety officers is less easy than for people working on a production line. With non-repetitive activities, it is perhaps better to compare total labour costs with an overall departmental budget based upon past experience of the work involved.

In order to obtain the maximum control benefits from pre-set performance standards, care must be taken that the standards have been properly set. It is also important that deviances from planned activities are quickly and thoroughly analysed, so that the necessary corrective measures can be taken whilst there is time to influence activities.

A STEP FURTHER

Daff, *Cost and Management Accounting*. Woodhead Faulkner, Ch. 3.
Drury, *Management and Cost Accounting*. Van Nostrand Reinhold, Ch. 3.
Lucey, *Costing*. D.P. Publications, Chs 7 and 8.
Norkett, *Management Accounting*. Pitman, Ch. 4.
Riddle, *Stage I Costing*. Northwick, Ch. 3.

Chapter 6

Overheads: collection, classification, allocation and apportionment

---

GETTING STARTED

The previous two chapters have looked at accounting methods for those expenses which can be traced readily to the cost centre: direct materials and direct labour. *Indirect* expenses are those which cannot be readily identified with output, and which therefore demand some *conventional* approach to accommodate them within the costing records.

It is necessary to be clear about the problems which indirect costs present, and about the reasons for, and the nature of, the methods used to overcome these problems.

Discussive questions tend to examine:

(1) The problems which indirect costs present, and why.
(2) The reasons behind the various methods that can be used to overcome these problems.
(3) The definition of terms such as *allocation*, *apportionment*, and *absorption* of overheads.

Computational questions take the form of calculating:

(1) The overhead to be allocated – or apportioned – to departments.
(2) The overhead to be absorbed by production.
(3) The production cost of items or processes made up of prime cost and overheads.

ESSENTIAL PRINCIPLES

Overheads can be classified into:

- **indirect materials** – cleaning equipment and materials, cooling oils, light tools, stationery, packing materials.
- **indirect labour** – wages and other staffing costs of maintenance, managerial, clerical, cleaning, administrative, research and security personnel.
- **indirect expenses** – rent, rates, insurance.

Some indirect expenses can be identified with specific production departments: depreciation of equipment, and plant maintenance; metered gas, water and electricity; and office stationery.

Unusual items, such as losses arising from wastage or faulty production, are usually excluded; so too are losses from obsolescence, income taxes, bonuses payable under profit-sharing schemes, and dividends payable to shareholders. Each of these special items is usually transferred to separate accounts for monitoring and control.

Cost allocation refers to the charging of discrete, identifiable items of cost to cost centres or cost units. Direct costs can be allocated to cost centres because, by definition, they are easily traceable. Some indirect costs, also, can be allocated to departments, as when fuel is metered.

Where, however, indirect costs are shared by two or more cost centres, estimates of these indirect costs must be *apportioned* amongst the cost centres on some acceptable basis. There are no strict rules here; the basis chosen should be appropriate, and should be equitably applied.

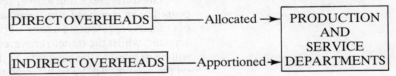

Examples of bases used for apportionment include:

Table 6.1

Expense	Method of apportionment
Welfare, canteen, safety	Number of workers; direct labour hours; wages bill
Depreciation of plant and buildings; fire insurance; rates	Capital values of plant and buildings
Lighting, heating, rent	Departmental floor areas
Works management expenses; inter departmental services	Direct labour hours
Electricity, water, gas, oil, steam, heating, air conditioning	Technical estimates

With each of the above, the department is apportioned a percentage of the estimated service costs depending upon its proportion of the total floor area, capital value, etc.

The calculation is the same irrespective of the basis upon which the costs are to be apportioned:

- First, calculate each department's proportion of the base's total: note that when using percentages the total of all the percentages should always add to 100.
- Second, apply these percentages to the overhead being apportioned.
- Third, check the answers by adding the overhead apportioned to ensure that *all* of the overhead has been dealt with.

USE OF ESTIMATES

Often, the actual indirect expenses will not be known until the end of an accounting period – three months or a year. Companies, therefore, establish estimates of the likely level of indirect expenses, and apportion these *estimated* costs amongst the departments. The alternative would be to delay sending out bills until all costs were known, and this would clearly be unacceptable.

OVERHEAD ADJUSTMENT ACCOUNT

Where overhead recovery is based upon estimates, it is very unlikely that the amount recovered during the period will exactly match the amount of overhead incurred. There will almost certainly be an *over recovery* of overheads – where more is recovered than was spent – or an *under recovery* – where less was recovered than was spent.

The differences due to over recovery or under recovery will be posted to an *overhead adjustment account*: the over recovered overheads representing a form of profit, and being credited to the account, whilst the under recovered overheads represent a loss, and will be debited to the account. At the end of the period, the balance on the account will be transferred to the Profit and Loss account, showing either that more was recovered than was incurred – a form of profit; or showing that less was recovered than was incurred – a form of loss.

APPORTIONING SERVICE DEPARTMENTS' OVERHEADS TO PRODUCTION DEPARTMENTS

At this stage, *all* departments, production and service departments have had overheads apportioned to them. But all overheads have to be covered by the revenue generated by the production departments, so that all of the service departments' overheads must be apportioned to the production departments.

Sometimes, this can be done on the basis of the records kept by the service departments of work done for production; in other cases, some short investigation may be mounted to ascertain the most equitable way of apportioning the expenses. Usually, the service departments' expenses are apportioned on the basis of percentages (Fig. 6.1).

Fig. 6.1

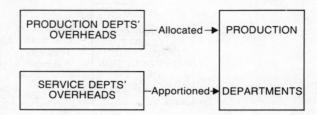

| INTER-SERVICE TRANSFERS | Where service departments make use of each others' facilities, the apportioning of costs is more involved. Three methods are commonly used: |

1. Elimination method.
2. Continuous allotment.
3. Algebraic method (simultaneous equations).

Elimination method

Select that service department with the largest overhead costs, and apportion the costs as normal. Next, take the second service department's costs and apportion as normal. When adding the total costs for the production departments, that part of the second service department's overheads which have gone towards the first service department are *ignored*.

Remember, the apportionment of overheads to production is based upon estimates and accounting conventions. To say therefore that the elimination method is giving an inaccurate result by ignoring figures in this way is to misunderstand the assumptions underlying the conventions being used.

Continuous allotment method

This method begins by allotting the agreed percentages to each of the service departments in turn. After the first round, however, only the *increases* are allotted in the agreed percentages. The allotment continues between the departments until the amount being allotted becomes too small to be significant.

Algebraic method

The algebraic method makes use of simultaneous equations, through which can be found the two unknowns – the overheads for the two service departments.

OVERHEAD ABSORPTION

Once the overheads have been apportioned, they must be *absorbed* into the production costs of the relevant departments. Overheads are absorbed by means of *overhead absorption rates*. These rates tend to be based either upon direct labour hours – or upon machine hours – depending upon the nature of the production processes (Fig. 6.2).

Fig. 6.2

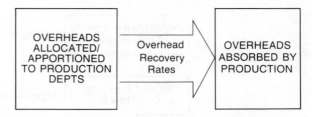

To calculate the rates, the total estimated overhead for a production department is divided by the number of direct labour hours – or the number of machine hours – which is thought the department will work during the period. Once the hourly rate has been calculated, the costs of any job passing through the department will have an element of overhead costs added; the amount of the overhead costs being based upon the number of direct labour hours – or the number of machine hours – incurred on it.

USEFUL APPLIED MATERIALS

Overhead costs may be used not simply to determine the cost of a good or service: they may also be used as part of the basis for determining funding. In the county of Cambridgeshire, for example, the amount of money a college receives per year is based upon an agreed lecturer cost plus overheads.

Courses are grouped according to four classifications: Group 1 – laboratory based; Group 2 – classroom based; Group 3 – Art and Design; and Group 4 – Secretarial. Overheads as a percentage of the lecturer cost are added to give a cost per teaching group. This figure is then divided by the agreed ratio of staff-to-students, to give a cost per full-time student equivalent. Once agreed, a college's finances for the year depend upon how many students of each category it enrols. Additional payments are made for exceptional factors, as agreed.

Fig. 6.3 Unit cost statement

XYZ College of Further Education

College Budget

	Unit Cost Budgeting			
	Group I	Group 2	Art & D	Secretarial
Lecturer cost 1987–1988 (£)	14,000	14,000	14,000	14,000
Overheads Add for non-teaching costs				
Group I 67%	9,380			
Group 2 41%		5,740		
Art & D 67%			9,380	
Secretarial 67%				9,380
	2,3380	19,740	23,380	23,380
Divide by Target SSRs	9.06	10.64	9.2	10.64
Unit Cost	2,580	1,855	2,541	2,197

					TOTAL
Application of Unit Costs:					
FTE Students	1,100	700	150	100	2,050
Multiplied by Unit Costs gives a budget of (£)	2,838,000	1,298,500	381,150	219,700	
					4,737,350

Note: The figures are for illustration only.

Source: Cambridgeshire County Council

RECENT EXAMINATION QUESTIONS

Question **1** examines those factors which influence overhead absorption practices: the question is the subject of the *Tutor's Answer*. Question **2** looks at the differences for overheads absorbed and those incurred, and asks how these are to be handled. Questions **3**, **4**, and **5** look at different aspects of the calculation of overhead apportionment and absorption. Question **6** examines inter service transfers.

1

(a) Outline briefly the process of charging indirect costs to cost units.
(6 marks)

(b) What are the factors which should influence how the costs of internal services in an organisation are passed on to the users of those services? Illustrate your answer.

(11 marks)

(ACCA Level 1, December, 1985)

2

(a) When budgeted rates are used to absorb overheads into product costs, in the month or short period it is unlikely that the overhead absorbed will equal the overhead incurred.
   Discuss the reasons for the difference.

(b) However, over the year it is likely that absorbed and incurred overhead will be nearly equal. If they are not nearly equal describe the factors that have caused the inequality.

(c) State the steps to be taken in the accounting system to deal at the end of a short period with:
   (i) an expected difference;
   (ii) an unexpected (or exceptional) difference.

(16 marks)
(RSA Stage III, June, 1984)

3 The following data relate to the three production cost centres of a factory:

	Machining	Assembly	Painting
Average number of employees	240	80	80
Kilowatt-hours (thousands)	400	50	50
Values of stores issued (£000)	120	40	20
Floor areas (000 square metres)	40	24	16
Machine hours (thousands)	120		
Direct man hours (thousands)		70	40
Budgeted overhead (£000)	221.4	85.8	30.8

Budgeted costs of the four *service* cost centres are:

	(£)
Material supply	18,000
Personnel	16,000
Heating	10,000
Power	20,000

(i) Apportion the budgeted costs of the service cost centres over the production cost centres, using suitable bases of apportionment.

(12 marks)

(ii) Ascertain the total overhead of each production cost centre.

(2 marks)

(iii) Calculate overhead absorption rates.

(6 marks)
(LCC Intermediate, Summer 1986)

4 The machine shop of a small factory houses three machines. The overhead costs of the machine shop have been budgeted for the year 1986–87 as follows:

	(£)	(£)
Repairs:		
Drilling machine	1,290	
Capstan lathe	1,140	
Cutting machine	400	
		2,830
Rent and rates		1,680
Power		5,600
Heating and lighting		1,260
Depreciation (machines)		7,000
Insurance (buildings)		1,400
Insurance (machines)		1,050
Canteen and welfare		1,680
		22,500

The following particulars relate to the machines:

	Drilling Machine	Capstan Lathe	Cutting Machine
Area occupied (sq. metres)	100	200	50
Number of personnel	3	2	2
Running hours	3,600	1,800	1,800
Horse power	10	5	10
Book value	£45,000	£30,000	£30,000

Apportion the budget costs over the three machines and calculate a machine-hour absorption rate for each machine.

(20 marks)
(LCC Higher, Spring, 1986)

5

(a) A company absorbs overheads by means of budgeted departmental rates. The rates used are as follows:

Production departments	Rate
Machine shop	120 per cent of direct wages incurred
Finishing shop	80 per cent of direct wages incurred
Assembly	£0.126 per unit of output

Non-production department	
Stores issued	125 per cent of direct materials

The following was recorded in week 49:

Department	Materials charged (£)	Wages incurred (£)	Overhead charged (£)
Machine shop	1,936	4,800	5,785
Finishing shop	11,616	6,300	4,735
Assembly	5,808	1,800	7,555
Stores			24,570

Units manufactured – total 58,500

Calculate for each department and in total:

(i) the amount of overhead absorbed into costs, and

(6 marks)

(ii) the amount of over or under absorbed overheads

(6 marks)

(b) The overheads absorbed by the non-production department requires secondary allocation to the production departments.

From the required information given in (a) above, recommend a way in which allocation may be achieved.

You must show supporting calculations stating the amount to be absorbed by the production departments.

(7 marks)

(AAT Level 3, December, 1985)

6 The budgeted overhead for the coming year allocated to the three production departments and two service departments of a manufacturing company were:

Production department:	A	120,000
	B	150,000
	C	90,000
Service department:	D	81,000
	E	57,000

After a study, it was decided that the costs of the service departments should be apportioned as follows:

		Service	department
		D (%)	E (%)
Production department:	A	—	40
	B	60	30
	C	30	25
Service department:	D	—	5
	E	10	—

You are required to calculate the total overhead attributable to each of the production departments by each of the following three methods:

(a) Ignoring the service that each of the two service departments gives to the other.

(5 marks)

(b) Using a method of apportionment whereby:
  (i) the cost of the service department that serves most departments is apportioned first; and
  (ii) the cost of the other service department is then apportioned to the production departments only.

(5 marks)

(c) Using the 'repeated distribution' or 'continuous allotment' method of apportioning the costs of the service departments among the production and the two service departments.

(10 marks)

(RSA Stage III, April, 1986)

OUTLINE ANSWERS

2

(a) Differences may arise because the level of output, the direct labour hours worked – or the machine hours worked – are different from what was anticipated. If more hours are worked, then more overhead will be recovered: if fewer hours are worked, less overhead will be recovered.

(b) If, over the whole period, absorbed overhead is markedly different from incurred overhead, then the basis upon which it is being absorbed may require reconsideration, since the basis is proving to be unsatisfactory. It may be that the basis for apportioning overheads is unsuitable, or that the recovery based upon (say) labour hours does not adequately reflect the true position. It may also be that the estimate of likely overheads to be incurred during the period has proved to be inaccurate.

(c) (i) Expected differences of small amounts may be transferred to the Overhead Adjustment account, and carried down as a balance on this account, in the hope that the balance may be removed during future periods. At the end of the main accounting period, the balance on the Overhead Adjustment account will be transferred to the Profit and Loss account.

(ii) Unexpected differences may be transferred straight to the Profit and Loss account, where the unusual nature of the difference can be revealed.

3

(i)–(ii)

Table 6.2

	Machining (£000)	Assembly (£000)	Painting (£000)	Total (£000)
Materials supply	12.0	4.00	2.00	18.00
Personnel	9.60	3.20	3.20	16.00
Heating	5.00	3.00	2.00	10.00
Power	16.00	2.00	2.00	20.00
	42.60	12.20	9.20	64.00
Budgeted overhead	221.40	85.80	30.80	338.00
Total overhead	264.00	98.00	40.00	402.00

The costs of materials supply have been apportioned on the basis of value of stores issued; personnel costs have been apportioned on the basis of average number of employees; heating on the basis of floor area; and power on the basis of kilowatt-hours. Note that a 'Total' column has been included in the table, to act as a check during the calculation: at each stage, the figures should be added across to the total, to ensure that no errors have been made.

Once the service departments' overheads have been apportioned, the *budgeted overheads for the production departments* themselves need to be brought into reckoning: many candidates will have omitted to do this, and will have worked part (iii) on the basis of the service departments' figures only.

(iii) Overhead absorption rates:

$$\frac{264}{120} \qquad\qquad \frac{98}{70} \qquad\qquad \frac{40}{40}$$

£2.2 £1.4 £1.0
per machine hour per direct labour hour

The total overheads for each production department are divided by the total of machine hours – in Machining – and by the total of direct man hours – in Assembly and Painting.

4 A question very similar to (**3**) above; only a skeletal working is shown (Table 6.3).

Table 6.3

Apportionment		Drilling machine (£)	Capstan lathe (£)	Cutting machine (£)	Total (£)
Repairs	Actual	1,290	1,140	400	2,830
Rent etc.	Area	480	960	240	1,680
Power	Horse power	2,240	1,120	2,240	5,600
Heating etc.	Area	360	720	180	1,260
Dep. – mach.	Book value	3,000	2,000	2,000	7,000
Ins. – bldgs	Area	400	800	200	1,400
Ins. – mach	Book value	450	300	300	1,050
Canteen	No. personnel	720	480	480	1,680
		8,940	7,520	6,040	22,500
Machine hour rate		£2.483	£4.178	£3.356	

5

(a) (i)–(ii)

	Machine shop (£)	Finishing shop (£)	Assembly (£)	Stores (£)
Overhead absorbed	5,760	5,040	7,371	24,200
Overhead charged	5,785	4,735	7,555	24,570
Over absorbed overhead		305		
Under absorbed overhead	25		184	370

(b) Recommend that the stores overheads be apportioned to the production departments on the basis of materials charged. Thus:

	Machine shop (£)	Finishing shop (£)	Assembly (£)	Stores (£)
Budgeted overhead	5,760	5,040	7,371	24,200
Allocation of stores overheads	2,420	14,520	7,260	—
	8,180	19,560	14,631	

6

(a)

	Production depts			Service depts	
	A (£000)	B (£000)	C (£000)	D (£000)	E (£000)
Budgeted overhead	120	150	90	81	57
Service dept D	—	49	24	—	(8)
	120	199	114	—	—
Service dept E	23	17	14		
				(3)	—
	143	216	128		

(b) This is the *Elimination Method* referred to in the text.

	Production depts			Service depts	
	A (£000)	B (£000)	C (£000)	D (£000)	E (£000)
Budgeted overhead	120	150	90	81	57
Service dept D	—	49	24	—	8
	120	199	114	—	65
Service dept E	26	20	16		
				(3)	—
	146	219	130		

Note that under this method the 5 per cent of E's expenses going to D is ignored (£3): only £62 of E's overhead is apportioned: £26 + £20 + £16 = £62.

(c) The *Continuous Allotment Method*.

	Service department	
	D (£000)	E (£000)
Initial overhead	81.0	57.0
10% of D to E		8.1
		65.1
5% of E to D	3.3	
	84.3	
10% D's *increase* to E		0.3
		65.4
5% of E's *increase* to D	0.02	
	84.32	

The figures now become too small to be meaningful: the total overheads apportioned to D are thus £84,300; and to E £65,400. These figures are now apportioned to the production departments:

	Production depts			Service depts	
	A (£000)	B (£000)	C (£000)	D (£000)	E (£000)
Budgeted overhead	120	150	90	84	65
Service dept D	—	51	25	—	(8)
	120	201	115	—	65
Service dept E	26	20	16	(3)	—
	146	221	131		

Note that the overheads for D and E are apportioned to the production departments, but that the inter-departmental apportionment is ignored; this has already been done in deriving the figures of £84 and £65.

The accuracy of the calculation can be checked by adding the total amount apportioned to the production departments: £146 + £221 + £131 = £498. This was the amount of overhead that had to be apportioned at the beginning: £120 + £150 + £90 + £81 + £57 = £498.

A TUTOR'S ANSWER

1

(a) Overhead cost is the total cost of indirect materials, indirect labour, and indirect expenses. Indirect costs are those which cannot be charged directly to the product or service. Thus, the cost of supervision cannot be charged directly to individual items of production, and is therefore classified as an indirect labour cost. Coolants and cleaning materials are examples of indirect materials: plant insurance and rates are examples of indirect expenses.

Whilst overhead costs may not be chargeable directly to *units of production*, some overhead costs may be chargeable directly to a particular *department*, as when fuel is metered. Such overhead costs can be *allocated* in total to the individual production or service departments.

Those indirect costs which cannot be charged directly to departments – either production or service departments – demand the use of some acceptable method of apportionment; and since the *actual* costs may not be known until after the accounting period, estimates of cost must be used. Thus, the estimated cost of heating for the period may be apportioned on the basis of a department's floor area; the estimated cost of welfare services may be apportioned on the basis of the numbers employed within each department. There is no hard and fast rule: any reasonable basis for apportionment is acceptable.

Once overheads have been allocated/apportioned to the production and service departments, the total of the service departments' overheads can be apportioned to the production departments, again using some acceptable basis such as floor area, hours of work done, etc. At the end of this procedure, all of the organisation's overheads are being carried by the production departments.

It remains only to absorb the overheads into production on the basis of an agreed *overhead absorption rate*. Where the production tends to be labour intensive, a rate per direct labour hour may be used: where output is machine intensive, a rate per machine hour may be more appropriate. The total overheads carried by a production department is divided by the estimated number of direct labour hours (or machine hours) to be worked, to obtain an overhead recovery rate per hour. All work passing through the department will therefore have added to its cost an element for overheads based upon the number of direct labour hours (or machine hours) expended upon it.

Because overhead absorption rates may be based upon estimates – estimates of actual overheads, and estimates of the number of direct labour or machine hours to be worked – it is likely that the company will recover more for its overheads than it spends – *over absorption of overheads* – or less – *under absorption*. Such differences may be transferred to an *Overhead Adjustment Account*, the balance of which is transferred to the Profit and Loss Account at the end of the period. Over absorbed overhead represents a form of profit: under absorbed overhead represents a form of loss.

(b) The way in which the costs of internal services are passed on will depend upon whether the cost centre is of a production or administrative nature. It will also depend upon the type of service: is it a one-off, or is it repetitive? Are there clear input–output relationships within a cost centre? Do users have a choice of using the service? Is it worthwhile developing a sophisticated system to monitor the cost transfers?

Examples might include the Maintenance department, and the Personnel department. Maintenance has close links with the production areas, and indeed, maintenance costs may be directly traceable to particular jobs. A form of job costing may therefore be introduced for particular machines. Thus, because of the close relationship between production and maintenance, efforts to improve the accounting treatment of overhead costs here are likely to improve the quality of information and management decision-making.

With the Personnel department, activities are further removed from production, and it is less easy to identify clear input–output relationships. Because of this, efforts to improve the way in which the Personnel department's costs are passed on to different users are less likely to improve efficiency or the quality of decision-making.

Other factors which may influence the treatment of overheads will be whether or not absorption or marginal costing methods are used, and whether overheads are absorbed on an actual or a predetermined basis.

A STEP FURTHER

Daff, *Cost and Management Accounting*. Woodhead Faulkner, Ch. 4.
Drury, *Management and Cost Accounting*. Van Nostrand Reinhold, Ch. 4.
Harvey and Nettleton, *Management Accounting*. Mitchell Beazley, Ch. 2.
Lucey, *Costing*. D.P. Publications, Ch. 9.
Riddle, *Stage I Costing*. Northwick, Ch. 3.

Chapter 7   Batch and job costing

GETTING STARTED

Questions on batch and job costing are popular with examiners, since within the scope of one question it is possible to examine a number of topics. Questions may test an understanding of direct wages, direct materials, and of overhead calculations, *as well as* testing an understanding of job and batch costing. Thus, before beginning to study this area of work, it is imperative that you have thoroughly understood the previous chapters: if you have any doubts, go back and re-read them.

Whilst many questions under this head will tend to be computational (as always with Cost and Management Accounting) discussive questions, or parts of questions are very common, testing knowledge of definitions, or depth of understanding.

Computational questions usually require the calculation of job, batch, or unit costs. Discussive questions tend to require:

(1) Definition of terms, such as job cost, batch production, etc.
(2) A description of accounting procedures.
(3) A comparison of job, batch, and contract costing, emphasising their salient features, and identifying their differences.

ESSENTIAL PRINCIPLES
PRODUCT COSTING

Product cost is the cost of an item built up from its cost elements:

$$\text{Product Cost} = \frac{\text{Direct}}{\text{Labour}} + \frac{\text{Direct}}{\text{Materials}} + \frac{\text{Direct}}{\text{Expenses}} + \text{Overheads}$$

The manner of determining product cost is greatly influenced by the nature of the production processes, and by custom and practice within an industry.

Where work comprises separate contracts, jobs, or batches – each of which is authorised by a special order or contract – *specific order costing* may be used. Where continuous processes are in operation, *process costing* will be adopted. The costing of specific services or functions involves *service costing*.

Product costing comprises:

- Specific order costing: job costing; batch costing; contract costing.
- Operation costing: process costing; service costing.

Remember, however, that whichever approach is adopted to collect and to calculate costs, the fundamental principles of determining costs still apply. What is different is the method of collecting and presenting the cost data.

Contract costing is discussed in Chapter 8; process costing is dealt with in Chapter 9; and service costing in Chapter 10.

JOB COSTING

Job costing applies where work is undertaken to a customer's special requirements, and where each order is of comparatively short duration. This is in comparison to *contract costing*, where work is undertaken to a customer's specific requirements, but where the work is of comparatively *long* duration.

Job costing may be used by garages, where the work on each customer's car becomes a separate job; made-to-measure tailors and dressmakers, too, may use job costing.

Usually, each job will be given an identifying number, and a *job card*. All costs relating to the job will be coded to the job number, and entered on the job card, so that a job cost can be calculated. In this way the company can identify the costs actually incurred by a particular job, and can ensure that the expenses are properly allocated. This is especially important where the selling price is determined by adding a percentage onto the cost price to allow for profit.

BATCH COSTING

Batch costing applies where similar articles are produced in groups, and where each group maintains its identity throughout one or more stages of production. Effectively, each batch becomes a 'job' for costing purposes. Thus, bakeries, potteries, etc. tend to use batch costing.

USEFUL APPLIED MATERIALS

Fig. 7.1 shows a job sheet for a printer. The sheet will carry the job order number, and the labour hours – inclusive of the overhead element – for each department: the codes after the departmental names refer to the departmental accounting codes. The materials used are listed separately, and the total cost of the job entered at the bottom of the sheet.

Fig. 7.1

OUTWORK

Contractor (206) _____

Order No. _____

				Paper				Materials
			Stock No.	Sheets	@	Per.		
HOURS		Camera Room (203)	£					
Est.	Act.							
			£					
		Machine Room (201)		Plates/Negatives No./Type				
					@			
					@			
					@			
			£	Standing				
		Finishing Room (202)		Machine _____				
				3m plates _____				
				Tape. _____				
				Comb. _____				
				Slide. _____				
			£					
		Guillotine (202)					£	
			£			%	£	
		Packing (202)				Total	£	
			£			Rank Xerox		
		Rank Xerox (205)				TOTAL MATERIALS		
			£					
		Total Labour						
		TOTAL						

Source: Howard Shinn Printing

Question **1** tests an awareness of the benefits of job costing, and of the information procedures necessary to operate such a system. Questions **2**, **3**, and **4** involve the calculation of job costs. Question **5** also involves a calculation of job cost, but the answer is a little more complicated, and it has therefore been selected for the *Tutor's Answer*.

1 The management of a large manufacturing company are considering introducing a system of job costing into their Plant Maintenance and Repair department. At present all the expenses incurred by this department, which is regarded as a service function to the production departments, are collected and apportioned to the production departments under the expenses heading 'General Works Expenses'.

(a) Describe the benefits to the company which may result from introducing a job costing system into the Plant Maintenance and Repair department.

(9 marks)

(b) Outline the information and procedures required in order to establish the total cost of individual repair or maintenance jobs.

(8 marks)

(ACCA Level 1, June 1985)

2 Electronic equipment is manufactured and supplied to customers' special requirements. Job No. AB985 has been completed and supplied at the agreed price of £850 and the following cost details shown in Table 7.1 are on record:

Table 7.1

Direct Materials:

Code	Quantity	Price
NB217	200 kg	£0.50 kg
CL110	4 units	£21.00 each
X814	55 metres	£0.40 per metre
Paint	6 litres	£3.00 per litre

Direct Labour:

Dept	Hours	Hourly rate (£)	Production Overhead Rate per direct labour hour (£)
1	30	3.20	2.50
2	20	3.50	2.75
3	10	3.10	2.90

Administration overhead is absorbed on the basis of 10 per cent of total production cost, whilst 4 per cent of the selling price is allowed for selling overhead. Delivery to the customer costs £48.00.

Prepare a job cost sheet showing prime cost, production cost, total cost, and profit (or loss).

(20 marks)

(LCC Intermediate, Spring, 1985)

3 Work is carried out to customers' special requirements by BCD Limited. Job No. 231 was in progress on 30 April, when accumulated costs were materials £900, wages £288 and overhead £258.

The following costs were charged to jobs in May:

Job No.:	231	232	233
Materials (£)	216	864	1,242
Wages (£)	720	1,080	630

Overhead expenditure in May amounted to £2,250 but jobs were charged at the pre-determined rate of 90 per cent of direct wages. The following two jobs were completed in May:

Job No.	Contract Price
231	£3,550
232	£3,475

(i) Ascertain the cost of each job to 31 May.

(10 marks)

(ii) Ascertain the profit earned in May, taking under absorbed overhead into account.

(10 marks)

(LCC Intermediate, Summer, 1986)

4 A type of metal bracket is made in batches of 500 on a machine. Batch No. 42 was machined at a rate of 10 per hour. 100 units failed to pass inspection. Of these, 60 were judged to be rectifiable and the remainder were scrapped. Rectification work took 6 hours (machine work).

The following details applied:

Raw material per unit	1 kg @ £1.40
Scrap value per bracket	£0.75
Machinist's hourly rate	£4.0
Machine-hour overhead rate (running time only)	£3.0
Setting up Machine (wages) – normal machining	£25.0
– rectification	£17.0

(i) The cost of a full batch, in total and per unit, if all units pass inspection.

(5 marks)

(ii) The actual cost of Batch No. 42, in total and per unit, after crediting the recovery value of the scrapped components and including the rectification costs.

(8 marks)

(iii) The loss incurred as the result of defective work.

(7 marks)

(LCC Higher, Spring 1986)

5 In order to identify the costs incurred in carrying out a range of work to customer specification in its factory, a company has a job costing system. This system identifies costs directly with a job where this is possible and reasonable. In addition, production overhead costs are absorbed into the cost of jobs at the end of each month, at an actual rate per direct labour hour for each of the two production departments.

One of the jobs carried out in the factory during the month just ended was Job No. 123. The following information has been collected relating specifically to this job:

400 kg of material Y were issued from stores to Department A: 76 direct labour hours were worked in Department A at a basic wage of £4.50 per hour. Six of these hours were classified as overtime at a premium of 50 per cent.

300 kg of material Z were issued from stores to Department B. Department B returned 30 kg of material Z to the storeroom being in excess to requirements for the job.

110 direct labour hours were worked in department B at a basic wage of £4.00 per hour. Thirty of these hours were classified as overtime at a premium of 50 per cent. All overtime worked in department B in the month is a result of the request of a customer for early completion of another job which had been orginally scheduled for completion in the month following.

Department B discovered defects in some of the work, which was returned to Department A for rectification: 3 labour hours were worked in department A on rectification (these are additional to the 76 direct labour hours in Department A noted above). Such rectification is regarded as a normal part of the work carried out generally in the department.

Department B damaged 5 kg of material Z which then had to be disposed of. Such losses of material are not expected to occur.

Total costs incurred during the month on all jobs in the two production departments were as follows:

	Department A (£)	Department B (£)
Direct materials issued from stores	6,500	13,730
Direct materials returned to stores	135	275
Direct labour at basic wage rate†	9,090	11,200
Indirect labour, at basic wage rate	2,420	2,960
Overtime premium	450	120
Lubricants and cleaning compounds	520	680
Maintenance	720	510
Other	1,200	2,150

Materials are priced at the end of each month on a weighted average basis. Relevant information of material stock movements during the month, for materials Y and Z, is as follows:

	Material Y	Material Z
Opening stock	1,050 kg (value £529.75)	6,970 kg (value £9,946.50)
Purchases	600 kg @ £0.50 kg 500 kg @ £0.50 kg 400 kg @ £0.52 kg	16,000 kg @ £1.46 kg
Issues from stores	1,430 kg	8,100 kg
Returns to stores	—	30 kg

This includes in Department B the scrapped material Z. This was the only material scrapped in the month.

† All direct labour in Department A is paid a basic wage of £4.50 per hour, and in department B £4.00 per hour. Department A direct labour hours included a total of 20 hours spent on rectification work.

(a) Prepare a list of the costs that should be assigned to Job No. 123. Provide an explanation of your treatment of each item.

(17 marks)

(b) Discuss briefly how information concerning the cost of individual jobs can be used.

(5 marks)

(ACCA Level 1, December 1985)

OUTLINE ANSWERS

1

(a) The benefits of introducing a job costing system include a knowledge of actual costs of the repair and maintenance work. This is useful when comparing options to replace plant; it also encourages production managers to consider the cost of repairs before calling in the maintenance department, since the cost of the repairs can be set against specific departments. It may also encourage managers to embark upon preventative maintenance, and to instil into their work force a more responsible attitude to the equipment under their control. Whilst the cost of repairs is charged as an overhead, there is little direct incentive to improve matters. Better knowledge of repair costs may lead to the calculation of more realistic overhead absorption rates, since the cost of the Maintenance department can be more accurately charged to production.

Experience in calculating actual costs could then be used as a basis for developing estimates for particular maintenance tasks; this information will help in deciding whether to carry out work with the firm's own work force, or whether to call in outside contractors. The information may also be used in deciding whether particular items are worthy of repair.

Once estimated costs have been established, a budgetary control system can be introduced, along with a standard costing system, so that variances between estimated and actual costs can be examined. (See Chapter 13 below for standard costing.)

(b) The procedure needed to collect the costs of particular repairs will demand that each job be given a job card, showing the job's unique number or code, and upon which all the costs relating to that job can be recorded. Material requisition and return notes will need to be coded with the job's code, so that the necessary entries can be made upon the job card. Similarly, workers' time sheets will need to record time spent upon each job. Overhead costs will need to be recovered using some pre-agreed absorption rate, possibly based upon the direct labour hours spent upon the job. Note, too, that in the calculation of the overhead absorption rates, those indirect services enjoyed by the Maintenance department will need to be included: the costs of the Safety department, for example, may be partly borne by the Maintenance department.

2

Materials	(£)	Labour	(£)	Prod O/H	(£)
NB217	100	Dept 1	96	Dept 1	75
CL110	84	Dept 2	70	Dept 2	55
X814	22	Dept 3	31	Dept 3	29
Paint	18				
	224		197		159

	(£)	(£)	(£)
Selling price			850
Prime cost (£224 + £197)	421		
Production overhead	159		
Total production cost		580	
Administrative overhead (10% × £580)		58	
Selling overhead (4% × £850)		34	
Delivery		48	
Total cost			720
Profit			130

3
(i)

	Job No.		
	231	232	233
	(£)	(£)	(£)
Accumulated costs: £900 + £288 + £258	1,446	—	—
May's costs: Materials	216	864	1,242
Wages	720	1,080	630
Overheads (90% wages)	648	972	567
Total cost	3,030	2,916	2,439

(ii)

	(£)	(£)
Contract price (£3,550 + £3,475)		7,025
Less expenses: Materials (£216 + £864 + £1,242)	2,322	
Wages (£720 + £1,080 + £630)	2,430	
Overheads (as actually incurred)	2,250	
		7,002
Profit accruing		23

This is made up of:

	(£)	(£)
Profit on Job 231 (£3,550 − £3,030)	520	
Profit on Job 232 (£3,475 − £2,916)	559	
		1,079

Less:

	(£)	(£)
Difference in opening and closing accumulated expenses (£2,439 − £1,446)	993	
Under absorbed overhead (£2,250 − £2,187)	63	
		1,056
Profit		23

4
(i)

	Unit cost (£)	Total cost (£)
Raw materials	1.40	700
Wages (machinist's hourly rate £4.0 × 50 hours)	0.40	200
Overheads (machine time 50 hours × overhead rate £3.0)	0.30	150
Setting up costs	0.05	25
Costs of full batch of 500 units	2.15	1,075

(ii)

	(£)	(£)
Cost of full batch		1,075
Rectification costs:		
Wages (6 hours machine work @ £4.0 hour)	24	
Overheads (6 machine hours × £3.0)	18	
Set up costs	17	
		59
Total cost		1,134
Less income from scrapped components		
(40 × £0.75)		30
Total cost of 460 units		1,104

Cost of the batch per unit: £1,104 ÷ 460 = £2.40

(iii)

	(£)
460 units should have cost 460 × £2.15	989
Actual cost	1,104
Loss incurred through defective work	115

A TUTOR'S ANSWER

This question may appear difficult at first sight, largely because of the sheer amount of reading necesary. The question is, however, reasonably straight forward if it is broken down into its constituent parts. It tests an understanding of job costing, an ability to calculate and to apply overhead absorption rates, and an awareness of how to handle abnormal costs within particular circumstances.

5

(a) In order to calculate the cost of Job No. 123, it is necessary to calculate the material, labour, and the overhead costs separately, and then to bring them together to strike a final cost.

   Material costs: Materials are priced at the end of the month on a weighted average basis. The formula to use is:

$$\frac{\text{Value of opening stock } + \text{ Value of purchases}}{\text{Quantity of opening stock } + \text{ Quantity of purchases}}$$

   For Y the costs are:

$$= \frac{£529.75 + £300 + £250 + £208}{1,050\,\text{kg} + 600\,\text{kg} + 500\,\text{kg} + 400\,\text{kg}}$$

$$= \frac{£1,287.75}{2,550\text{kg}}$$

$$= £0.505\,\text{kg}$$

Since 400 kg of Y went to Job 123, the cost is 400 kg × £0.505 = £202

For Z the costs are:

$$\frac{£9,946.50 \ + \ £23,360}{6,970\,\text{kg} \ + \ 16,000\,\text{kg}}$$

$$= \qquad \frac{£33,306.50}{22,970\,\text{kg}}$$

$$= \qquad £1.45\,\text{kg}$$

Job 123 had issued to it 300 kg of Z, but 30 kg were returned, and 5 kg were damaged: the amount of Z going to the job was therefore 300 − 30 − 5 = 265 kg. The cost was 265 × £1.45 = £384.25.

Labour costs: In Department A direct labour hours were 76 normal plus 3 rectification. Of these, 6 hours were overtime: it would be unfair to charge a particular job with the overtime premium, since just which job is being worked on during overtime hours has to do with work scheduling. It is probably better, therefore, to charge the premium to overhead, to be borne by all jobs going through the department. The labour costs in A are therefore 76 hours at £4.50 per hour: £342.

In Department B 110 hours were spent on the job, but of these 30 hours were overtime worked because of another customer's requirements. The overtime premium here will be charged to this other job. The direct labour costs of Department B will be 110 hours at £4.00 per hour, giving £440.

Overhead costs: The rectification work in A is to be regarded as overhead – 20 hours × £4.50 hour = £90. The cost of the scrapped items, however, is regarded as an abnormal cost, and is excluded from the overhead calculation. The overtime premiums in A are to be included as agreed above, but the overtime worked in B was for another job, and will therefore be excluded from these calculations.

| | Overheads (£) | |
	A	B
Rectification – labour	90	—
Indirect labour	2,420	2,960
Overtime premium – Dept. A	450	—
Lubricants and cleaning compounds	520	680
Maintenance	720	510
Other	1,200	2,150
	5,400	6,300

Overheads are to be absorbed using an actual rate per direct labour hour for each department. Total direct labour hours worked can be calculated by dividing the direct labour costs by the basic hourly rate:

Department A $\qquad \dfrac{£9,090 - £90}{£4.50} \qquad = \quad 2,000\,\text{hours}$

Note that the £90 of rectification work is deducted from A's labour costs here.

Department B $\qquad \dfrac{£11,200}{£4.00} \qquad = \quad 2,800\,\text{hours}$

The overhead absorption rates per direct labour hour are thus:

Department A $\qquad \dfrac{£5,400}{2,000\,\text{hours}} \qquad = \quad £2.70$

Department B $\qquad \dfrac{£6,300}{2,800\,\text{hours}} \qquad = \quad £2.25$

Total costs:

Using the results of the above calculations, it is now possible to compute the cost of Job No. 123:

	(£)	(£)
Direct materials:		
Material Y 400 kg × £0.505 kg	202.00	
Material Z 265 kg × £1.45 kg	384.25	
		586.25
Direct labour:		
Department A 76 hours × £4.50 hour	342.00	
Department B 110 hours × £4.00 hour	440.00	
		782.00
Overheads:		
Department A 76 hours × £2.70 hour	205.20	
Department B 110 hours × £2.25 hour	247.50	
		452.70
Total cost		1,820.95

(b) Information on individual job costs can be used for valuing work-in-progress; assessing the profitability of specific jobs; and comparison with estimates given before the job was undertaken. Such comparisons will act as a test of the efficiency and accuracy of the estimating activity within the organisation.

A STEP FURTHER

Daff, *Cost and Management Accounting*. Woodhead Faulkner, Ch. 5.
Drury, *Management and Cost Accounting*. Van Nostrand Reinhold, Ch. 5 for job costing: Ch. 6 for batch costing.
Lucey, *Costing*. D.P. Publications, Chs 11 and 12.
Norkett, *Management Accounting*. Pitman, Ch. 3.
Riddle, *Stage I Costing*. Northwick, Ch. 4.

Chapter 8

Contract costing

GETTING STARTED

Contract costing is a form of specific order costing, where work is undertaken to a customer's specific instructions and where each order is of a long duration, usually lasting for more than a year. This is in contrast to job costing, where work is also undertaken to a customer's specific order, but where the work tends to be of a short duration.

Discussive questions tend to cover:

1. Definition of terms such as contract costing, notional profit, and retention money.
2. Comparison of contract costing with job, batch, and process costing.
3. Justification for retention money and for notional profit calculation.

Computational questions comprise:

1. Compilation of contract account.
2. Calculation of retention money, and of profits.

ESSENTIAL PRINCIPLES
CONTRACT ACCOUNT

Each contract will be allocated a contract number, and all expenses incurred on the contract will be charged to that number on a contract cost account. This will act much as the job card in job costing, except that with contracts, because they tend to run over a long period, the detailed entries will tend to be more numerous, and possibly more complicated.

The contract account will record the direct materials, direct wages, and overheads relevant to the contract. But, because by their very nature contracts tend to run over more than one accounting period, the contract account will often contain opening and closing stocks of materials sent to the site, wages owing, and expenses owing or prepaid.

An outline of a contract account presented in vertical form might be as shown in Table 8.1:

Table 8.1   *Contract Account*

	(£000)	(£000)
Materials		XXX
Wages		XXX
Depreciation		XXX
Sub contractors' charges		XXX
Head office expenses		XXX
		XXX
Add opening Work-in-progress		XXX
Less closing Work-in-progress		XXX
Total cost (A)		XXX
Value of work certified	XXX	
Less total cost (A)	XXX	
Notional profit		XXX
Profit taken (using formula)	XXX	
Profit in suspense	XXX	
Notional profit		XXX

A common expense in such contracts is depreciation on plant and machinery. In many questions, the figure for depreciation is not given directly. Instead, the value of plant on hand at the beginning of the contract may be stated, along with the value of plant on site at the end of the period. The relevant amount of depreciation can be calculated by subtracting the two figures:

$$\text{Depreciation} = \frac{\text{Value of plant at start}}{\text{of period, or contract}} - \frac{\text{Value of plant at end}}{\text{of period or contract}}$$

It is important to be aware of the difference between the *cost* of work completed, and the *value* of work completed:

the cost of work done appears at cost price;
the value of work done appears at 'selling price';
the difference between the two represents a *notional profit*.

WORK-IN-PROGRESS

When a company undertakes a contract for a client, the client will probably employ their own agents to certify that various stages or parts of the work have been carried out in accordance with the agreed specification. When agreement is reached upon the standard and nature of the work completed, the agent will issue a certificate showing that the contractor is entitled to stage payments under the terms of the contract. Such payments are normally credited by the contractor to the contract account.

Any work which has been done, but which has not been certified, appears by way of work-in-progress. Where a contract spreads over three accounting periods, there will be both opening and closing work-in-progress.

PROFITS

It is in the calculation of profit on contracts that complications may arise. Following the doctrine of prudence, profits on contracts should not be taken until the contract is completed. This, however, would distort the contractor's profit reporting, since little or no profit would accrue in periods whilst work was in progress; and large profits would be reported in other periods, simply because a number of contracts had come to completion. Thus, with long contracts, extending over more than one accounting period, a *prudent* profit figure is usually recorded.

Either one of two formulae may be used to calculate profits on uncompleted contracts. In the first formula, although not required by SSAP 9, the use of the fraction emphasises the degree of prudence in profit-taking.

- $\text{Profit} = \frac{2}{3} \times \text{Notional profit} \times \frac{\text{Cash received}}{\text{Work certified}}$

Or,

- $\text{Profit} = \frac{\text{Work certified}}{\text{Contract price}}$

SSAP 9

SSAP 9 on the valuation of stocks and work-in-progress directs that no profit shall be taken on a contract until the outcome of the contract can *reasonably* be foreseen. Whereas all losses must be reflected in the accounting statements as soon as they occur. Of that profit which can reasonably be foreseen, only that proportion which *prudently* reflects the work done to date should be regarded as being earned to date. The method of taking up these profits should be *consistently* applied from one period to another.

SSAP 9 also insists that in calculating such profits, due allowance should be made for the estimated costs of any rectification, and any future work to be undertaken under the contract. Due allowance should also be given for likely increases in the level of future costs.

In calculating the profit for a particular period, allowance must be made for that proportion of likely profit which has been taken in previous years.

Note that Schedule 4, paragraphs 22 and 23 of the 1985 Companies Act requires that the amount to be shown in respect of any current asset shall be its purchase price or production cost, or net realisable value if lower. However, the requirement that every balance sheet and profit and loss account shall show a 'true and fair view' overrides Schedule 4 of the act. See the *Tutor's Answer* on p. 96.

RETENTION MONEY

Under the terms of some contracts, certain payments are withheld by way of *retention money*. Retention money represents an agreed proportion of the contract price which is withheld by the client for an agreed period after the completion of the work. The money acts as security against the contractors should they fail to carry out their obligations under the contract. Thus, with building work, 15 per cent of the agreed price may be withheld for 12 months to see whether any defects might result from the work.

Where retention money applies, the profit on uncompleted contracts should be reduced accordingly. Thus, where the retention is 15 per cent of the agreed price, any profit figure calculated using the above formulae would be reduced by 15 per cent.

That part of the notional profit which is not taken as profit is put to suspense, and continues as a balance on the contract account until the end of the contract, when a final profit is struck.

BALANCE SHEET ENTRIES

Because the contract extends over more than one accounting period, the value of plant, the stocks of materials and of work-in-progress, the prepayments, and accruals, will all appear on the balance sheet. All of the items mentioned will appear as assets, except the accruals.

The only item which may cause difficulty is that of the work-in-progress. In examinations, the balance sheet entry for work-in-progress may appear:

	(£000)	(£000)
Work-in-progress	XXX	
Profit taken to date	XXX	
	XXX	
Less cash received on account	XXX	
		XXX

USEFUL APPLIED MATERIALS

In practice, contract accounts may be kept in many different forms. The example given in Fig. 8.1 shows a contract account kept on a micro computer. The account shows the contract number; a description of the job; the budget; date for completion; an indicator showing whether the contract is overdue, completed, or ongoing; cost codes for the expenses incurred; descriptions of the individual costs; the source of the cost, e.g. purchases ledger, labour, etc.; the dates and references of each transaction; the units and amounts involved; the percentage added to each expense to recover overheads, and the total 'uplifted' cost, i.e. cost plus overhead; comments against each expense; a summary by cost type; totals excluding and including invoices; and an overall summary.

Fig. 8.1

Pegasus Software

18.04.84 — Job Cost Report — Page 4

Cost Summary

	B/Forward	Current	Total	Uplifted	B/F Units	Current	Total Units
Materials	694.22	339.00	1033.22	1291.53	0.00	0.00	0.00
Skilled Labour	33.88	19.25	53.13	59.48	11.50	7.00	18.50
Semi-Skilled Labour	9.75	63.14	72.89	81.60	5.00	30.00	35.00
Total Invoiced	-700.00	-700.00	-1400.00	-1400.00	0.00	0.00	0.00
Plant Hire	0.00	35.00	35.00	42.00	0.00	0.00	0.00
Total Including Invoices	37.85	-243.61	-205.76	74.61	16.50	37.00	53.50
Excluding Invoices	737.85	456.39	1194.24	1474.61			

J005 Swimming Pool at The Limes, Wilford — Budget 15250 — By 25 Aug 83 Overdue

Code	Source	Date	Reference	Units	Amount	Overhead	Uplifted	
P05 Pump Hire	Cost	20.07.83	65239	0.00	65.00	% 10.0000	71.50	Pump for s'fce water
L03 Lorry Driver (Normal Time)	Labour	20.07.83	A003	1.00	2.50	% 11.9500	2.80	-
L04 Lorry Driver (O/Time 1)	Labour	20.07.83	A003	1.50	4.28	% 11.9500	4.79	-
S05 Plumber (Normal Time)	Labour	20.07.83	B001	2.00	5.50	% 11.9500	6.16	-
S06 Plumber (O/Time 1)	Labour	20.07.83	B001	1.00	3.85	% 11.9500	4.31	- Overtime
P05 Pump Hire	Cost	20.07.83	PH/45812	0.00	35.00	% 10.0000	38.50	1 day pump hire
S05 Plumber (Normal Time)	Labour	18.04.84	B001	2.00	5.50	% 11.9500	6.16	-
S06 Plumber (O/Time 1)	Labour	18.04.84	B001	1.00	3.85	% 11.9500	4.31	- Overtime
L03 Lorry Driver (Normal Time)	Labour	18.04.84	C001	2.00	5.00	% 11.9500	5.60	General
M01 Site Materials	Cost	12.04.84	12331/1	0.00	17.21	% 25.0000	21.51	Fillers
M01 Site Materials	Cost	12.04.84	12331/1	0.00	522.00	% 25.0000	652.50	Tiles
P05 Pump Hire	Cost	18.04.84	PH/45812	0.00	35.00	% 10.0000	38.50	1 day Pump Hire
S05 Plumber (Normal Time)	Labour	18.04.84	B001	2.00	5.50	% 11.9500	6.16	-
S06 Plumber (O/Time 1)	Labour	18.04.84	B001	1.00	3.85	% 11.9500	4.31	- Overtime
Invoice	Invoice	15.02.84	4566	0.00	-120.00		-120.00	Services Invoice

Cost Summary

	B/Forward	Current	Total	Uplifted	B/F Units	Current	Total Units
Plant Hire	100.00	35.00	135.00	148.50	0.00	0.00	0.00
Semi-Skilled Labour	6.78	5.00	11.78	13.19	2.50	2.00	4.50
Skilled Labour	18.70	9.35	28.05	31.41	6.00	3.00	9.00
Materials	0.00	539.21	539.21	674.01	0.00	0.00	0.00
Total Invoiced	0.00	-120.00	-120.00	-120.00	0.00	0.00	0.00
Total Including Invoices	125.48	468.56	594.04	747.11	8.50	5.00	13.50
Excluding Invoices	125.48	588.56	714.04	867.11			

Pegasus Software

18.04.84 — Job Cost Report — Page 5

Overall Summary

	B/Forward	Current	Total	Uplifted	B/F Units	Current	Total Units
Materials	1606.48	4448.34	6054.82	7568.55	130.00	0.00	130.00
Semi-Skilled Labour	66.16	291.02	357.18	399.86	29.00	138.00	167.00
Skilled Labour	159.26	344.40	503.66	563.86	53.00	111.75	164.75
Plant Hire	476.50	1547.12	2023.62	2372.52	0.00	0.00	0.00
Total Invoiced	-700.00	-5061.00	-5761.00	-5761.00	0.00	0.00	0.00
Total Including Invoices	1608.40	1569.88	3178.28	5143.79	212.00	249.75	461.75
Excluding Invoices	2308.40	6630.88	8939.28	10904.79			

Source: Job Costing Manual. Pegasus Software Limited

RECENT EXAMINATION QUESTIONS

Question **1** is a discussive question touching on the nature of contract costing, and requiring a comparison with job costing. Questions **2**, **3**, and **4** are calculation questions requiring the compilation of a contract account, with adjustments for notional profits. Question **5** is also a contract account question, but because it is more involved, it has been selected for the *Tutor's Answer*.

1

(i) Define 'specific order costing'.

(5 marks)

(ii) Give three examples of industries in which job costing would be applied.

(4½ marks)

(iii) Give three examples of industries in which contract costing would be applied.

(4½ marks)

(iv) Specify three ways in which the work undertaken by industries using contract costing usually differs from that undertaken by those using job costing.

(5 marks)

(LCC Intermediate, Spring, 1986)

2 KL Constructors PLC obtained a contract (No. 72) to build a Sports Centre for a price of £1,500,000, the agreed date of completion being 31 December 1985. Work commenced on 10 September 1984. The company's financial year ended on 31 May 1985 and on that date the following balances appeared in the accounts relating to the contract:

	(£000)
Wages paid	140
Materials issued to site	320
Materials returned from site	30
Hire of plant	150
Own plant on site at valuation on 10/9/84	200
Supervision	46
Head office charges	120
Value of work certified	800
Cost of work completed but not yet certified	80
Cash received	660

On 31 May 1985:

(i)   The company's own plant was revalued at £180,000.
(ii) Wages due but unpaid amounted to £4,000.
(iii) Unused material on site was valued at £50,000.

Prepare the account for Contract No. 72 for the period from 10 September 1984 to 31 May 1985 showing the amount of profit to be carried to the company's main Profit and Loss Account, and the amount of profit to be held in suspense to cover contingencies.

(20 marks)
(LCC Intermediate, Summer, 1985)

3 A civil engineering company constructing a multi-storey car park had the following balances in the contract account at the close of the last accounting period:

	£000's
Materials on site	35
Plant on site	360
Sub contractors' charges not received	18
Work completed but not certified	30

The details on p. 90 apply to the contract for the next accounting period.

	(£000's)
Materials issued to site	207
Materials on site at the end of period	20
Wages paid	141
Wages accrued	16
Plant sent to site	110
Plant valuation carried forward	400
Sub contractors' charges	87
Sub contractors' charges not received	11
Head office charges	27
Cash received from client	540
Value of work certified	600
Value of work completed but not certified	36

(a) The contract account showing clearly the profit for the period transferred to Profit and Loss Account.

(18 marks)

(b) A Balance Sheet showing appropriate entries from the contract account.

(4 marks)

(AAT Level 3, June, 1985)

4   EFG Constructions PLC is building an office block for UK Developments PLC, work having commenced in September 1984. The financial year of EFG Constructions ended on 30 April 1985, at which date the contract was still in progress and the following information appeared in the accounting records:

	(£000)
Direct materials:	
issued to contract	400
returned to central store	10
transferred to other contracts	15
on site 30 April 1985	25
Direct wages:	
paid on site	250
accrued at 30 April 1985	10
Direct expenses:	
paid on site	30
accrued at 30 April 1985	5
Cash received from contractee	840
Cost of work not yet certified	70
Invoice value of work certified	960
Plant installed (at cost)	120
Plant on site (revalued 30 April 1985)	90
Allocation of company overhead	175

From the above information, prepare the contract account to 30 April 1985 as it would appear in the books of EFG Constructions PLC, clearly showing:

(i)   the 'apparent profit';
(ii) the profit to be taken for the financial year;
(iii) the opening entries for the year commencing 1 May, 1985.

(20 marks)

(LCC Higher, Summer 1985)

5 AB PLC, contractors and civil engineers, are building a new wing to a hospital. The quoted fixed price for the contract is £3 million. Work commenced on 7 January 1985, and is expected to be completed on schedule by 30 June 1986. The company's financial year ended on 31 March 1986 and it is company policy to apply the requirements concerning long-term contracts which are contained in SSAP 9 on Stocks and Work-in-Progress.

Data relating to the contract at 31 March 1986:

During the fifteen months to 31 March:

	(£000)
Plant sent to site at commencement of contract	240
Hire of plant and equipment	77
Materials sent to site	662
Materials returned from site	47
Direct wages paid	960
Wage-related costs	132
Direct expenses incurred	34
Supervisory staff salaries – direct	90
– indirect	20
Regional office expenses apportioned to contract	50
Head office expenses apportioned to contract	30
Surveyors' fees	27
Progress payments received from Health Authority	1,800

The following points are to be considered:

1. Plant is to be depreciated at the rate of 25 per cent per annum, straight line basis, with no residual value.
2. Unused materials on site at 31st March are estimated at £50,000.
3. Wages owed to direct workers total £40,000.
4. No profit in respect of this contract was included in the year ended 31 March 1985.
5. Budgeted profit on the contract is £800,000.
6. Whilst the contract is expected to be completed by the scheduled date without encountering difficulties, it is obvious to the management that the budgeted profit will not be realised. However, to calculate the attributable profit to date you are to assume that further costs to completion will be £300,000.

(a) (i) Prepare the account for the hospital contract for the fifteen months ended 31 March 1986.

(12 marks)

(ii) Show the work-in-progress valuation as it will appear in the company's balance sheet at 31 March.

(3 marks)

(iii) Calculate the profit on the contract by one other method, taking a more prudent view than that advocated in SSAP 9 and assuming for **this part of your answer** that the cost of work **not** certified is £500,000 and that the invoice value of work certified is £2 million. (Show clearly any formulae you use and your workings.)

(6 marks)

(b) Explain and comment on the following statement which was printed in the 'Notes on Accounts' section of the 1983 published accounts of the contracting company:

'In accordance with the provisions of SSAP 9 the attributable profit amounting to £8,048 (1982: £303,357) is included in the value of long-term contracts. The inclusion of this attributable profit is a departure from the statutory valuation rules for current assets but is required to enable the accounts to give a true and fair view.'

(4 marks)

(CIMA Stage 2, Specimen, 1985)

OUTLINE ANSWERS

1

(i) Specific order costing is the costing method applicable where work consists of separate contracts, jobs or batches, each of which is authorised by a special order or contract.

(ii) Examples are industries that carry out short-term work to a customer's instructions. Thus, garages repairing vehicles, jobbing builders, printers, painters and decorators, tailors and dressmakers, specialised engineering companies, upholsterers, etc.

(iii) Examples are industries that carry out work to the customer's instructions, but where the work is of long duration. Thus, civil engineering companies, contract builders, shipbuilders, aircraft manufacturers etc.

(iv) The work tends to be for a longer period, giving rise to the existence of opening and closing stocks of raw materials and work-in-progress; the need to certify work actually completed, so that profit can be allowed as the work progresses; the existence of staged payments for work done; the use of retention monies, as a guarantee against future rectification.

KL Constructors PLC
Contract No. 72

	(£000)	(£000)
Materials issued to site	320	
Less returned	30	
	290	
Less on site 31/5/85	50	
		240
Wages paid	140	
Add due	4	
		144
Hire of plant		150
Own plant issued to site	200	
Less plant value at 31/5/85	180	
		20
Supervision		46
Head office charges		120
		720
Less work not certified (W.I.P.)		80
Total cost		640
Value of work certified	800	
Less total cost	640	
Notional profit		160
Profit taken	88	
Profit in suspense	72	
		160

Profit calculation: $\frac{2}{3} \times £160 \times \frac{£660}{£800} =$ £88

3

(a)   *Multi-Storey Car Park*
                                       Contract Account

	(£000)	(£000)
Materials on site at start of period	35	
Add issued	207	
	242	
Less on site at end of period	20	
		222
Wages paid	141	
Add accrued	16	
		157
Plant on site at start of period	360	
Add plant sent to site	110	
	470	
Less plant valuation carried forward	400	
		70
Sub contractors' charges paid	87	
Less owing for previous period	18	
	69	
Add outstanding this period	11	
		80
Head office charges		27
		556
Add Work-in-progress at beginning of period		30
		586
Less Work-in-progress at end of period		36
Cost of work done		550
Value of work certified	600	
Less cost of work done	550	
Notional profit		50
Profit taken	30	
Profit to suspense	20	
		50

(b)

Balance Sheet (Assets section)

	(£000)	(£000)
Plant on site		400
Materials on site		20
Work-in-progress (£560 + £36 + £24)	620	
Less cash received	540	
		80

Balance Sheet (Liabilities section)

	(£000)	(£000)
Sub contractors' charges	11	
Wages owing	16	
		27

4

(i)

EFG ConstructionPLC
UK Developments PLC Contract

	(£000)	(£000)	(£000)
Direct materials:			
issued		400	
Less: returned	10		
transferred	15		
		25	
		375	
Less on site 30 April		25	
			350
Direct wages: paid on site		250	
add owing		10	
			260
Direct expenses: paid on site		30	
add owing		5	
			35
Plant installed at cost		120	
Less value @ 30 April		90	
			30
Company overhead			175
			850
Less cost of work not yet certified			70
Cost of work certified			780

95

Invoice value of work certified			960
Less cost of work certified			780
Apparent profit (notional profit)			180

(ii)

Profit to Profit and Loss account		105
Profit in suspense		75
		180

(iii)

Work not certified	Dr	70
Materials on site	Dr	25
Plant on site 30 April 1985	Dr	90
Profit in suspense		75
Wages owing		10
Expenses owing		5

A TUTOR'S ANSWER

5

(a) (i) *Hospital Contract Account*

	(£000)	(£000)	(£000)
Plant depreciation (£240 × 25% × 1.25)		75	
Hire of plant		77	
Materials		662	
Direct wages	960		
add accrued	40		
		1,000	
Wage-related costs		132	
Direct expenses		34	
Supervisory staff: direct	90		
indirect	20		
		110	
Regional office expenses		50	
Head office expenses		30	
Surveyors' fees		27	
			2,197

Less:

	(£000)	(£000)
Materials on site, 31st March 1986	50	
Materials returned	47	
		97
Cost of work to date		2,100

(ii) *Work-in-Progress*

	(£000)	(£000)
Cost of work to date	2,100	
Attributable profit	525	
Work-in-progress		2,625

The attributable profit is calculated as follows:

	(£000)	(£000)
Price of contract		3,000
Cost to date	2,100	
Further estimated cost	300	
		2,400
Estimated profit		600

The amount of the estimated profit attributable to the fifteen months to 31 March 1986 is:

$$\text{Estimated profit} \times \frac{\text{Cost of work completed}}{\text{Total estimated cost}}$$

$$£600,000 \times \frac{£2,100,000}{£2,400,000} = £525,000$$

Work-in-progress valuation for the balance sheet is thus;

	(£000)	(£000)
Cost to date	2,100	
Attributable profit	525	
		2,625
Less cash received		1,800
		825

(iii) The formula normally used to ascertain profit on uncompleted contracts is:

$$\tfrac{2}{3} \times \text{Notional profit} \times \frac{\text{Cash received}}{\text{Value of work certified}}$$

Notional profit is calculated:

	(£000)	(£000)
Value of work certified	2,000	
Cost of work not yet certified	500	
		2,500
Cost of work to date		2,100
Notional profit		400

Using the formula for ascertaining the profit, we obtain:

$$\frac{2}{3} \times £400 \times \frac{£1,800}{£2,000} = £240,000$$

(b) The emphasis in the 1985 Companies Act is upon a 'true and fair view'. Although the company in the question has included profits on uncompleted contracts as per SSAP 9, the 1985 Act requires that the amount to be included in respect of any current asset shall be its purchase price, its production cost, or its net realisable value, if lower. The rule has not been followed by the company, but this is allowable because the requirement that every balance sheet and profit and loss account shall show a 'true and fair view' is overriding. (Note that at the date shown in the question, reference to legislation should have been to the 1981 Companies Act.)

A STEP FURTHER

Black, *Accounting Standards*. Longman, Ch. 7.
Daff, *Cost and Management Accounting*. Woodhead Faulkner, Ch. 5.
Drury, *Management and Cost Accounting*. Van Nostrand Reinhold, Ch. 5.
Lucey, *Costing*. D.P.Publications, Ch. 13.
Norkett, *Management Accounting*. Pitman, Ch. 3.

Chapter 9

Process costing

Questions on process costing involve a number of concepts not met with in job, batch, or contract costing. Because the ideas are important for companies which use process costing, this area of the syllabus is popular with examiners.

Discussive questions tend to test:

1. The definition of terms.
2. Comparisons of the terms normal and abnormal losses; waste and scrap; joint products and by products.
3. A description of the necessary accounting procedures.
4. Comparisons of process costing with job, batch or contract costing.

Computational questions require:

1. The compilation of process accounts.
2. The calculation of gains and losses arising in manufacture.
3. The calculation of profits or losses upon the sale of scrap or rejects.
4. The calculation of work-in-progress in terms of equivalent units.

ESSENTIAL PRINCIPLES

PROCESS COSTING

Process costing applies where goods or services result from a series of continuous or repetitive operations. In such circumstances, individual units of output are not easily identified; the cost centre, therefore, becomes the process itself, rather than the unit of output. This is in contrast to job, batch, and contract costing, where the job, batch, or contract operate as the cost centre.

Thus, the costs of direct materials, direct labour, and of overheads are collected for each process, and are then averaged over the output of that process for the period in question.

A template for a process account kept in a *horizontal* form appears below. Notice that a record is kept, not just of the monetary values, but also of the physical quantities involved.

Process Account

	Units	(£)		Units	(£)
Opening WIP	XX	XX	*Normal loss*	XX	--
Trans from previous process	XX	XX	*Abnormal loss*	XX	XX
			Closing WIP	XX	XX
Costs incurred this process:			Trans. to next process	XX	XX
Direct materials		XX			
Direct labour		XX			
Production overhead		XX			
Abnormal gain		XX			
	XX	XX		XX	XX

A template for a process account kept in a *vertical* form would appear:

Process Account

	Units	Units	(£)	(£)
Balance b/d from previous period	XXX		XXX	
Transferred from previous process	XXX		XXX	
Direct materials			XXX	
Direct labour			XXX	
Production overhead			XXX	
Abnormal gain			XXX	
		XXX		XXX
Less: *Normal loss*	XXX		—	
Abnormal loss	XXX		XXX	
Balance c/d to next period	XXX		XXX	
		XXX		XXX
Transferred to next process		XXX		XXX

NORMAL LOSSES

In many processes, a certain proportion of the input material is lost simply through the normal process operations. Companies use their own experience to determine what the level of these losses ought to be. Expected losses incurred in this way are termed *normal losses* and are regarded as part of the legitimate costs of manufacture. Because of this, in the process account, although the number of units so lost is recorded, *the value of the units is not.*

The *exception* to this rule is where the normal losses can be sold: in such cases the monies received from the sale of normal losses are often credited to the process account so as to reduce the cost of production.

ABNORMAL LOSSES

Losses above those which would normally be expected are termed *abnormal losses*. They may arise because of poor raw materials, inefficient working, or faulty plant. In all cases, the occurrence of abnormal losses should be investigated by the firm's management.

To help in this, abnormal losses are usually credited to the process account, and are then transferred to a separate abnormal loss account. If the items are then sold, the monies received are usually credited to the abnormal loss account, and any balance is transferred to the profit and loss account.

Many candidates fail to calculate abnormal losses correctly. It is important to remember that rejected output incurs direct and indirect costs just as does good output. In valuing rejects therefore all these costs must be included.

ABNORMAL GAINS

Sometimes, a process may produce more units than would normally be expected. In these circumstances, *abnormal gains* arise. Such gains are debited to the process account. Clearly, abnormal losses and abnormal gains cannot arise on the same process account for the same period: either the process has produced more than was expected, or it has produced less.

Abnormal gains are also usually transferred to a separate account, since they too demand management's attention. It is as important to discover why expected output has increased, as it is to investigate why it has diminished. At the end of the period, the balance on the abnormal gains account represents a form of additional profit, and the balance is transferred to the credit of profit and loss account.

WASTE AND SCRAP

Waste is defined as discarded substances which have no resaleable value. Waste should be distinguished from *Scrap* which is discarded materials which do have some resaleable value. Sometimes, scrap can be sold just as it comes direct from the process, or it may be reintroduced into the process by way of raw material. Scrap iron arising from the smelting process is an example: it can be recycled into the furnace.

BY-PRODUCTS AND JOINT PRODUCTS

By-products are products which arise incidentally from the production of the main product. They have a saleable value which is *comparatively low* in relation to the main product. They may or may not require further treatment before being saleable.

Joint products also arise as a result of a common process, but here the value of the two products is *comparatively high*. Note, that what distinguishes by-products from joint products is the relative values of the products themselves.

Because joint products derive from common processes, the costs up to the point at which the products acquire their own identity are known as *joint costs*.

There are three methods of apportioning joint costs to the joint products:

1. Market value at point of separation.
2. Market value after further processing.
3. Comparison of physical quantities.

The first method is useful where further processing of the products incurs disproportionate costs, but obtaining market values may be difficult. The second method is easy to calculate, but gives inequitable results where the costs of further processing are disproportionate between the products. The third method assumes that each of the joint products is equally valuable (they may not be) and, of course, the method cannot be used where the products are measured in different forms – as with gases and solids.

WORK-IN-PROGRESS

The valuation of work-in-progress is often a difficult problem for process industries – and is a popular examination question with some examiners. The difficulty of valuing work-in-progress in process industries brings us to the concepts of *equivalent production* and *equivalent units*.

Equivalent units represent a *notional* quantity of completed units which is substituted for the actual units still in progress of manufacture. In practice, work-in-progress for each process is broken down into its cost elements; thus, a figure is derived for the degree of completion for direct materials, direct labour, and overheads. By using these figures, either in total or per element of cost, the value of work-in-progress can be calculated.

USEFUL APPLIED MATERIALS

Fig. 9.1 shows a cross section of a blast furnace used in iron making. The fuel and ore is charged at the top of the furnace, and the hot air blast is applied to the base. The main product here is the molten iron; but gas and slag are also produced as by-products. The gas may be sold to other industrial concerns, or to the nearby town; the slag may be sold for road making. All three products, however, emanate from the one smelting process.

Fig. 9.1   Iron making, product and bi-products

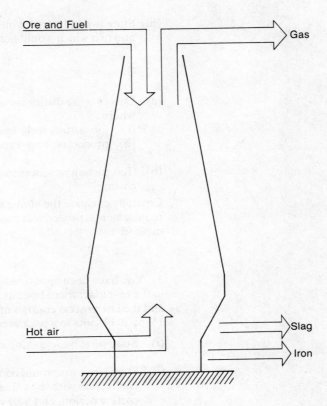

Iron making. Product and by-products

RECENT EXAMINATION QUESTIONS

Questions **1** and **2** touch on the differences between process costing and job costing. Question **3** requires you to examine the main features of process costing. Question **4** looks at joint products, and the 'split-off point'. Question **5** is concerned with the further processing of by-products; and Question **6** calls for the compilation of a process account, the handling of normal losses, and the valuation of work-in-progress. Question **7** deals with abnormal gains, and joint products; this question has been chosen for the *Tutor's Answer*.

1   AB Limited and BC Limited are both engaged in manufacture. Process costing is operated by AB Limited and job costing by BC Limited.

(i)   List three points of difference between the production features of AB Limited and those of BC Limited.

(9 marks)

(ii) Compare the respective methods of evaluating month-end work-in-progress in the two situations.

(7 marks)

(iii) State two industries which would normally use process costing and two which would normally use job costing.

(4 marks)

(LCC Intermediate, Summer 1985)

2

(a) Describe the distinguishing characteristics of production systems where
(i) job costing techniques would be used, and
(ii) process costing techniques would be used.

(3 marks)

(b) 'Job costing produces more accurate product costs than process costing.'

Critically examine the above statement by contrasting the information requirements, procedures and problems associated with each costing method.

(14 marks)

(ACCA Level 1, December 1984)

3 You have been appointed Cost Accountant to a company engaged in the manufacture of biscuits. There are ten different kinds of biscuit and the last process consists of packing them into film wrappings, 10, 15, or 20 biscuits to a pack according to brand.

(i) State what basic costing system you would expect to operate.

(2 marks)

(ii) State what you would consider would be the main difficulty in connection with the valuation of work-in-progress at the end of a costing period, and how you would deal with it.

(5 marks)

(iii) State what *cost unit* would be appropriate to each of the following processes:
(a) dough mixing;
(b) baking;
(c) packing in film.

(3 marks)

(iv) Assuming that the mixed dough is fed to a cutting operation where the individual biscuits take shape, state what you consider would be the most important control ratio in connection with the cutting operation, and why.

(5 marks)

(v) State whether or not the technique of *variance accounting* would be advantageous. Briefly give reasons for your preference.

(5 marks)

(LCC Higher, Autumn 1985)

4

(i) Define the term 'joint products'.

(4 marks)

(ii) Give three examples of industries where joint products arise.

(6 marks)

(iii) Explain briefly what is meant by:
(a) 'split-off' point;
(b) 'joint costs'.

(4 marks)

(iv) State the two most commonly used bases for apportioning joint costs to products.

(6 marks)

(LCC Higher, Summer 1985)

5 Since being ordered to refrain from discharging process waste effluent into the adjacent river, thus causing pollution, a chemical company has been filtering the effluent at a cost of £42 per kilolitre (1 kilolitre = 1,000 litres)

An alternative course of action is currently under consideration. This is to convert the effluent into a by-product, saleable as a weed killer concentrate, at £240 per kilolitre. The following particulars relate to one kilolitre of effluent;
Added chemical (UX 17), 200 litres at £0.36 per litre.
Processing costs £108.
Loss of fluid by evaporation, 100 litres.
Containers £36.
Marketing costs £30.

Prepare a cost statement showing the financial advantage or disadvantage (per kilolitre of *effluent*) which would result from adoption of the by-product scheme.

(20 marks)

(LCC Intermediate, Summer 1986)

6 A manufacturing company makes a product by two processes and the data below relate to the second process for the month of April. A work-in-progress balance of 1,200 units brought forward from March was valued, at cost, as follows:

	(£)
Direct materials, complete	10,800
Direct wages, 60% complete	6,840
Production overhead, 60% complete	7,200

During April, 4,000 units were transferred from the first process to the second process at a cost of £7.50 each, this input being treated as direct material within the second process.

Other costs incurred by the second process were:

	(£)
Additional direct materials	4,830
Direct wages	32,965
Production overhead	35,538

3,200 completed units were transferred to finished goods store. A loss of 520 units, being normal, occurred during the process. The average method of pricing is used.

Work-in-progress at the end of April consisted of 500 completed units awaiting transfer to the finished goods store and a balance of unfinished units which were completed as regards direct material and 50 per cent completed as regards direct wages and production overhead.

You are required to:

(a) Prepare for the month of April the account for the second process.
(14 marks)

(b) Present a statement for management setting out the:
  (i) cost per unit of finished product by element of cost and total;
  (ii) cost of production transferred to finished goods;
  (iii) cost of production of completed units awaiting transfer to finished goods;
  (iv) cost of uncompleted units in closing work-in-progress, by element of cost and in total.

(6 marks)
(CIMA Foundation, May 1985)

7 A company manufactures two types of industrial sealant by passing materials through two consecutive processes. The results of operating the two processes during the previous month are shown below:

Process 1
Costs incurred:

Materials 7,000 kg @ £0.50 per kg	£3,500	
Labour and overheads	£4,340	

Output:

Transferred to Process 2		6,430 kg
Defective production		570 kg

Process 2
Costs incurred:

Labour and overheads	£12,129	

Output:

Type E Sealant		2,000 kg
Type F Sealant		4,000 kg
By-product		430 kg

It is considered normal for 10 per cent of the total output from Process 1 to be defective and all defective output is sold as scrap at £0.40 per kg. Losses are not expected in Process 2.

There was no work-in-progress at the beginning or end of the month and no opening stocks of sealants.

Sales of the month's output from Process 2 were:

Type E Sealant	1,100 kg
Type F Sealant	3,200 kg
By-product	430 kg

The remainder of the output from Process 2 was in stock at the end of the month.

The selling prices of the products are Type E Sealant £7 per kg and Type F Sealant £2.50 per kg. No additional costs are incurred on either of the two main products after the second process. The by-product is sold for £1.80 per kg after being sterilised at a cost of £0.30 per kg, in a subsequent process. The opening costs of Process 2 are reduced by the net income receivable from sales of the by-product.

(a) Calculate, for the previous month, the cost of the output transferred from Process 1 into Process 2 and the net cost or saving arising from any abnormal losses or gains in Process 1.

(6 marks)

(b) Calculate the value of the closing stock of each sealant and the profit earned by each sealant during the previous month using the following methods of apportioning costs to joint products:
   (i) according to weight of output;
   (ii) according to market value of output.

(12 marks)

(c) Consider whether apportioning process costs to joint products is useful. Briefly illustrate with examples from your answer to (b) above.

(4 marks)

(ACCA Level 1, June 1985)

OUTLINE ANSWERS

1

(i) AB using process costing: units of output pass from one process to another, with no individual identity; labour and materials input cannot be related to particular items of product; overheads are charged to processes, and not to particular jobs. BC using job costing: units of output are clearly identifiable, and may be unique; labour and material costs are easily identified with work done; overheads are absorbed by individual jobs.

(ii) AB using process costing may base work-in-progress valuations upon the concept of equivalent units for each process; BC using job costing will identify direct materials, labour, and overheads going into individual jobs.

(iii) Process costing: cement manufacture, chemical production, some smelting operations, some food preparation activities. Job costing: builders, decorators, tailors, garages, home appliance repairers.

2

(a) Job costing: used where each job or order is a separate unit for cost purposes.
Process costing: used where the product passes through continuous processes; all units receive same treatment; usually difficult to identify one unit of output from another.

(b) Job costs: collected separately. Process costs: based upon averages. Would seem, therefore, that job costs might be more accurate.

But, whilst costing techniques re material pricing should not affect accuracy of figures – since both approaches rely upon material requisitioning procedures, and material pricing techniques – the situation re direct labour is not so straightforward.

In process costing, all of the cost of direct labour can be charged to the process; but, with job costing there is often an amount of 'waiting time' which cannot be traced to a particular job, and which must be charged to output by means of the less accurate overhead absorption rates.

Production overheads charged to output are based upon the usual mass of assumptions, and thus suffer from all of the inaccuracies normally encountered here. However, with process costing, many costs do not need to be treated as overheads since they can be charged direct to the process, whereas under job costing they would be included as overhead, and suffer from all of the problems normally associated with overhead apportionment and absorption.

Because job costing regards each job as unique, it usually demands much paperwork by way of material requisition notes, job tickets, etc. Because of this, mistakes are probably more likely with job costing than with process costing, where the paperwork may be comparatively straightforward.

Under process costing, there are problems over the need to estimate the degree of completion for assessing closing stock valuations; and in some cases the difficulties associated with joint products and by-products.

The occurrence of loss or waste should not effect the relative accuracy of the methods, since both methods demand the inclusion of allowances for normal wastage.

The calculation of an *average cost* per unit of output under process costing, rather than the calculation of a *specific cost* as in job costing, may suggest that job costing will be the more accurate here. However, assuming that all units pass through identical processes, the average cost should be an accurate measure.

In essence, therefore, it is not possible to assert that one method produces more accurate figures than does the other.

3

(i) Because the company operates ten different processes, suggest process costing: note, however, that some of the operations may lend themselves to batch costing, whilst others to process costing. A company may operate different forms of costing depending upon the nature of the technology.

(ii) Process costing: problems with assessing labour, material, and overhead input into semi-finished items. Suggest use of concept of 'equivalent production': explanation of 'equivalence'.

(iii) (a) kilogram or any unit relating to weight;
      (b) dozen biscuits, or gross (note use of *bakers' dozen*);
      (c) 100 packs, or by weight.

(iv) Comparison of number of good biscuits for a given weight of dough. This measure would help identify wastage, spoilage, or loss of material in manufacture. Note that production losses still incur direct costs and overheads.

(v) Variance accounting would be advantageous, since standards could be set – for each process – for materials, labour, and overhead inputs, and actual results compared with standards. In this way inefficient working could be identified, and remedied. (For a discussion of standard costing, see Chapter 13 below.)

4

(i) *Joint products* arise where two or more products are separated in the course of processing *and* each has a sufficiently high saleable value to merit recognition as a main product. Contrast with *by-products* which also arise from the same process as do main products, but which have comparatively low saleable values.

(ii) Examples of industries where joint products arise: the meat industry where different parts of the carcass may be used to produce different products; cokemaking, where gas, coke and chemicals may result from the same process; metal smelting, where gas may be produced, along with slag for road making, brick making, or cement manufacture. The oil and chemical industries also produce many joint products from common raw materials.

(iii) The *split-off point* – or *point of separation* – is that stage in the processing when joint products each acquire a separate identity. The stage in the processing when this occurs depends upon the processes and the products.
      Joint costs are those related to providing two or more products or services from common production processes. With joint products, the joint costs are those incurred up to the split-off point.

(iv) Joint costs may be apportioned using:
      (a) the market value at the point of separation;
      (b) market value after further processing;
      (c) physical measurement.

A discussion of the main features of any two of the above should prove acceptable. (See the main body of the text, p. 101.)

Weed Killer Concentrate

	(£)	(£)	(£)
Chemical (Ux17) £0.36 = 200	72.0		
Processing	108.0		
Containers	36.0		
Marketing costs	30.0		
		246.0	
Less saving on filtering costs		42.0	
Cost of 900 litres (allowing for evaporation)			204.0
Revenue from 900 litres (£240 × 900/1,000)			216.0
Profit			12.0

Note that if the weed killer concentrate is produced, there will be no need to filter the effluent before discharging it into the river: the saving of £42 per kilolitre must therefore be taken into account when assessing the weed killer alternative.

6

(a)

Second Process Account

	Units	Price (£)	Totals (£)	(£)
Work-in-progress b/fwd:	1,200			
Direct materials			10,800	
Direct wages			6,840	
Production overhead			7,200	
	1,200			24,840
Transfers from first process	4,000	7.5		30,000
Second process:				
Direct materials			4,830	
Direct wages			32,965	
Production overhead			35,538	
				73,333
	5,200			128,173
Normal loss	520			
Awaiting transfer to finished goods	500	29.45	14,725	
Work-in-progress:				
Direct materials	980	9.75	9,555	
Direct wages			4,655	
Production overhead			4,998	
	2,000			33,933
Items transferred to finished goods	3,200	29.45		94,240
	5,200			128,173

The work-in-progress is calculated:

$$\text{Total output} - (\text{normal loss} + \text{finished goods} + \text{finished goods awaiting transfer})$$

$$5,200 \quad - \quad (\quad 520 \quad + \quad 3,200 \quad + \quad 500 \quad)$$

$$= \quad \underline{\underline{980 \text{ units}}}$$

The number and value of output in equivalent units is:

	Equivalent units		
	Direct materials	Direct wages	Production overhead
Finished goods	3,200	3,200	3,200
Awaiting transfer	500	500	500
Unfinished goods	980	490	490
	4,680	4,190	4,190

Note that the unfinished goods were 50 per cent completed for wages and overhead.

	Cost per unit (£)		
	Direct materials	Direct wages	Production overhead
B/fwd from March	10,800	6,840	7,200
Input from Process 1	30,000		
Input during Process 2	4,830	32,965	35,538
	45,630	39,805	42,738

(b) (i)

Statement of Cost (£)

Direct materials	(£45,630 ÷ 4,680)	9.75
Direct wages	(£39,805 ÷ 4,190)	9.50
Production overheads	(£42,738 ÷ 4,190)	10.20
Total cost		29.45

(ii) Value of items transferred to finished goods: 3,200 × £29.45 = £94,240.

(iii) Value of items awaiting transfer: 500 × £29.45 = £14,725.

(iv) Cost of uncompleted items still in process:

Direct materials	980 × £9.75	9,555
Direct wages	980 × 50% × £9.50	4,655
Production overhead	980 × 50% × £10.20	4,998
		19,208

A TUTOR'S ANSWER

This question tests the ability to calculate the cost of output and of abnormal gain within process accounts. It also tests the ability to apportion process costs over joint products and to recognise the weaknesses of joint product cost apportionment.

7

(a)

Process 1

	(£)	(£)
Materials	3,500	
Labour and overheads	4,340	
		7,840
Less scrap value of normal loss (700 × £0.40)		280
		7,560
Normal output (90% × 7,000 kg)		6,300 kg
Normal cost per kg (£7,560 ÷ 6,300)		£1.20
Cost of output transferred to Process 2:		
(6,430 × £1.20)		£7,716

Net saving arising from abnormal gain

Savings from any abnormal increase in production must be reduced by the income normally derived from the sale of scrap at £0.40 kilo:

Abnormal gain = actual output − normal output	
= 6,430 kg − 6,300 kg	130 kg
Normal cost per kg	£1.20
Saving from abnormal gain (130 kg × £1.20)	£156
Deduct reduction in scrap value receivable:	
(130 kg × £0.40)	£52
Net savings	£104

(b)

Value of closing stocks

Cost of output: Process 2

Transferred from Process 1 (6,430 kg × £1.20)	7,716
Labour and overhead	12,129
	19,845
Less net realisable value of by-product:	
(430 × [£1.80 − £0.30])	645
	19,200

Values of closing stocks according to weight of output

Cost per kg produced: £19,200 ÷ 6,000 kg = £3.20 kg.
Value of closing stock:

Type E Sealant (2,000 kg − 1,100 kg) × £3.20	2,880
Type F Sealant (4,000 kg − 3,200 kg) × £3.20	2,560
Total value of closing stock:	5,440

According to market value of output

	Type E (£)	Type F (£)	Total (£)
Market value of output:			
(2,000 kg × £7.0)	14,000		
(4,000 kg × £2.50)		10,000	24,000
Cost of output			19,200
Cost of output as % of market value:			
(£19,200 ÷ £24,000) × 100 = 80%			
Market value of closing stock:			
(2,000 − 1,100 kg) × £7.0	6,300		
(4,000 kg − 3,2000 kg) × £2.50		2,000	8,300
Value of closing stock at cost:			
(£6,300 × 80%)	5,040		
(£2,000 × 80%)		1,600	6,640

Profit earned by sealants

Apportioning costs by weight of output

		Type E (£)	Type F (£)	Total (£)
Sales:	(1,100 × £7.0)	7,700		
	(3,200 × £2.50)		8,000	15,700
Cost of sales:	(1,100 × £3.20)	3,250		
	(3,200 × £3.20)		10,240	13,760
Profit (Loss)		4,180	(2,240)	1,940

The figure of £3.20 for cost of sales was derived from the closing stock calculations above.

Apportioning costs by market value

		Type E (£)	Type F (£)	Total (£)
Sales:	(1,100 × £7.0)	7,700		
	(3,200 × £2.50)		8,000	15,700
Cost of sales:	(1,100 × £7.0 × 80%)	6,160		
	(3,200 × £2.50 × 80%)		6,400	12,560
Profit		1,540	1,600	3,140

(c) Because process costs are arbitrarily apportioned to joint products, extreme care should be taken when using the results. In the answer above, the value of closing stock, and the amount of profit recorded depended simply upon the method chosen to apportion costs. Indeed, the weight of output method when applied to Sealant F values closing stock per kg at a higher figure than its market price: £3.20 kg as compared to £2.50 kg. This is unacceptable.

Type F Sealant appears to be unprofitable when using the weight of costs method; but appears to be the more profitable of the two products when using the market value method. Management, therefore, need to be careful about drawing conclusions from such calculations. Often, management will find it more useful to receive information which measures the profitability of the whole process, rather than that which purports to measure the profitability of particular joint products.

A STEP FURTHER

Daff, *Cost and Management Accounting*. Woodhead-Faulkner, Ch. 5.
Drury, *Management and Cost Accounting*. Van Nostrand Reinhold, Ch. 6 for process costing, and Ch. 7 for joint product and by-product costing.
Lucey, *Costing*. D. P. Publications, Ch. 15.
Norkett, *Management Accounting*. Pitman, Ch. 3.
Riddle, *Stage I Cost Accounting*. Northwick, Ch. 4.

Chapter 10　　　　　　# Service costing

GETTING STARTED

Service costing arises where specific functions or services are being costed rather than products or processes. Thus service costing has to do with activities such as transport, catering, the provision of steam, gas, etc. within a company. It also has to do with the provision of services by public utility organisations – gas, water, and electricity undertakings – and with the provision of social services such as health care.

Not all examination syllabuses include service costing. It is prudent therefore for you to check your own examination, and if service costing is included, ensure that you understand the elements of it, otherwise, your choice of question within the examination could be severely restricted.

The discussive questions look at the nature and purpose of service costing, and the application of service costing to particular situations. The computational questions usually require the compilation of a service cost account.

ESSENTIAL PRINCIPLES

SERVICE COSTING

With *service costing*, the cost unit – i.e. that quantity of service in relation to which costs are ascertained – varies depending upon the service. Thus, in hospitals, the cost unit may be based upon the beds occupied, or on the number of out-patients; with local authorities it may be per (£) of rateable value; schools and colleges may use the number of full-time equivalent students; transport organisations may use tonne-kilometres; passenger organisations may use passenger kilometres. Much depends upon the nature of the service being costed, and upon the uses to which the cost data are to be put.

Two examples of service activities, and the costs likely to be collected are given on p. 117.

With transport organisations, costs may be divided into:

(a) daily running costs – fuel, oil, grease, drivers' wages;
(b) maintenance costs – wear on tyres, servicing costs, spare parts, the hire of alternative transport whilst the company's own vehicles are off the road;
(c) fixed costs – insurance, vehicle taxes, depreciation, and possibly some part of the drivers' wages.

These costs are usually recovered from those departments which use the transport services. Such recovery is achieved by charging a rate per mile or per kilometre; or a rate per hour.

With catering operations, costs may be:

(a) provisions – food and drink;
(b) labour – cooks, waitresses, kitchen staff generally;
(c) services – fuel, power, heat and light, water;
(d) consumable items – linen, cutlery, crockery, cleaning materials, small cleaning tools such as brushes;
(e) fixed costs – rent, rates, insurances, depreciation.

There may also be income here to offset some of the expenses; monies received for meals and refreshments, counter sales, etc. The cost unit may be a meal served. Where the canteen is subsidised, so that costs exceed income, the deficit may be apportioned to the departments on the basis of the number of employees in those departments.

The service cost account

The various costs involved in providing the service will be recorded on a *service cost account*. Onto this account will be debited all the costs incurred; any income arising will be credited to the service cost account. The account will appear much as a job cost account.

USEFUL APPLIED MATERIALS

The *precise* layout of a service cost account will vary with the company concerned. Fig. 10.1 is a Summary Statement for use in hotels. *Note*, not only are the expenses included, but also the provision for budgeted totals, and for figures for the previous year. Such figures appearing upon a summary statement allow management to make useful comparisons.

Fig. 10.1 Summary Statement of Hotel Operations

Period ending _____ 19 ____

Survey, 'The UK Lodging Industry'
by Horwath & Horwath (UK) Ltd

	This year			
Total Revenue	Actual	Budget	Last year	Median %'s of total sales
Rooms dept. – Revenue				46.7
Payroll and related expenses				9.8
Other expenses				3.9
Total expenses				
Departmental profit				32.6
Food and beverage dept.				
Food revenue				29.6
Beverage revenue				16.0
Other income				
Total revenue				
Food cost				
Beverage cost				
Total costs				
Payroll and related expenses				16.1
Other expenses				2.8
Total expenses				
Departmental profit				11.3
Telephone/O.O. depts. (Note 1)				
Revenue		Telephone		2.3
		Other		2.1
Costs and expenses				
Profit (loss)				
Rentals/other income				
Income from operated depts				1.0
Administrative & general				
Payroll and related expenses				5.0
Other				
Total A & G				9.4
Marketing				
POMEC (Note 2)				1.4
Property Op./Maint		4.7		
		Energy		4.7
Total deductions				
Gross operating profit				23.4

Notes
1. O.O.Depts. – Other Operated Departments
2. POMEC – Property Operation, Maintenance and Energy Costs.

Source: (Thornfield: Accounting in Hotels: CIMA)

Question **1** is concerned with the purposes of service costing, and its application to a transport business. Questions **2** and **3** require the calculation of service costs; Question **3** has been selected for the *Tutor's Answer*.

1 B Limited owns a fleet of motor vehicles which it uses to deliver goods to its large retail stores.

(a) State the objectives of a cost accounting system which B Limited could use for its motor vehicle fleet.

(6 marks)

(b) Describe the nature of the records to be kept in the system referred to in (a) and indicate any analyses of the records that would be needed, giving examples of items included.

(10 marks)

(c) State whether or not you consider budgets or standards would be helpful in operating the system, and why.

(4 marks)

(RSA Stage III, May 1985)

2 John Walton uses four ten-tonne lorries in the operation of a delivery service. Each vehicle is expected to travel 15,000 kilometres per annum when loaded and the average load carried is expected to weigh 8 tonnes.

The budgeted total cost of operating the service for one year is £120,000 and profit is allowed for by adding 20 per cent to costs when invoicing customers.

On a certain day a load of 9 tonnes was accepted for delivery in two stages. At the first stop, 80 kilometres distant, 5 tonnes were unloaded and the remaining 4 tonnes were carried a further distance of 15 kilometres.

Calculate: (i) the charging rate per tonne-kilometre;

(10 marks)

(ii) the amount to be charged to the customer for the deliveries detailed above.

(10 marks)

(LCC Intermediate, Spring 1985)

3 The following information relates to two hospitals for the year ended 31.12.1985:

	St Mathew's	St Mark's
Number of in-patients	15,400	710
Average stay per in-patient	10 days	156 days
Total number of out-patient attendances	130,000	3,500
Number of available beds	510	320
Average number of beds occupied	402	307

Cost analysis

Patient care services	In-patients (£)	Out-patients (£)	In-patients (£)	Out-patients (£)
1. Direct treatment services and supplies (e.g. nursing staff):	6,213,900	1,076,400	1,793,204	70,490
2. Medical supporting services:				
(i) diagnostic (e.g. pathology)	480,480	312,000	22,152	20,650
(ii) other services	237,160	288,600	77,532	27,790
General services				
(i) Patient related (e.g. catering)	634,480	15,600	399,843	7,700
(ii) General (e.g. administration)	2,196,760	947,700	1,412,900	56,700

Note: In-patients are those who receive treatment whilst remaining in hospital. Out-patients visit hospital during the day to receive treatment.

(i) Prepare separate statements for each hospital for each cost heading:
  (a) cost per in-patient day, (£) to two decimal places;
  (b) cost per out-patient attendance, (£) to two decimal places.
  (8 marks)

(ii) Calculate for each hospital the bed-occupation percentage.
  (2 marks)

(iii) Comment briefly on your findings.
  (5 marks)
  (AAT, June 1986)

OUTLINE ANSWERS

1

(a) The objectives of a cost accounting system in such circumstances could include: a comparison of the costs of operating the firm's own fleet compared to contracting the work out, or hiring transport; the calculation of delivery costs to enable proper charges to be debited to the relevant stores; the calculation of charges should the company decide to hire out its own vehicles, and to enable comparisons to be made between the costs of operating different vehicles or class of vehicles.

(b) Cost information would need to be collected to enable a cost per mile – or per kilometre – to be calculated: the calculation of a cost per tonne would seem inappropriate here, since a wide variety of items are likely to be transported. These costs would be calculated for each individual vehicle using a form of vehicle log sheet. The log sheet would be completed by the driver to give information on journeys made, time taken; fuels, oils, etc. used; driver's time spent loading, unloading, driving; and details of waiting time, delays, etc.

(c) Standards would prove useful if regular journeys were allocated standard times; these would enable planned workloads to be better prepared, and would help to ensure that idle time was kept to a minimum. Variations from standard could then be identified and examined, in an effort to make the transport department more efficient.

2

(i)

Expected annual tonne-kilometres:

4 lorries × 15,000 kilometres each × 8 tonne average load = 480,000

Expected annual cost = £120,000

$$\text{Cost per tonne-kilometre} = \frac{£120,000}{480,000}$$

= £4.0 per tonne-kilometre

Charging rate per tonne-kilometre = £0.25 + 20%

= £0.30

(ii)   Amount to be charged to customer:

(£)

5 tonnes × 80 kilometres × £0.3 = 120

4 tonnes × 95 kilometres × £0.3 = 114

234

A TUTOR'S ANSWER

3

(i)   Cost per in-patient day and per out-patient attendance

	St Mathew's In-patients (£)	St Mathew's Out-patients (£)	St Mark's In-patients (£)	St Mark's Out-patients (£)
Direct treatment services	40.35	8.28	16.19	20.14
Medical supporting services:				
Diagnostic	3.12	2.40	0.20	5.90
Other	1.54	2.22	0.70	7.94
General services:				
Patient related	4.12	0.12	3.61	2.20
General	14.26	7.29	12.76	16.20
Total	63.39	20.31	33.46	52.38

The costs per in-patient day are found by dividing the individual cost headings by the number of patients *multiplied* by the average stay per in-patient. In the case of St Mathew's the costs are divided by 15,400 × 10 = 154,000; for St Mark's by 710 × 156 = 110,760.

The cost per out-patient attendance is merely the cost heading divided by the number of attendances.

(ii)

	St Mathew's	St Mark's
The bed occupation percentage =	$\dfrac{402 \times 100}{510}$	$\dfrac{307 \times 100}{320}$
	78.82%	95.94%

(iii) From the calculations, St Mark's long-stay patients cost less to treat than do the short-term patients at St Mathew's; in an answer, you should compare the salient cost differences. Discuss also the differing bed occupancy rates. It is likely that St Mark's treats more seriously ill patients than St Mathew's, but we cannot tell from the information given.

A STEP FURTHER

The following texts cover service costing generally:

Daff, *Cost and Management Accounting*. Woodhead Faulkner, Ch. 5.
Lucey, *Costing*. D. P. Publications, Ch. 14.
Norkett, *Management Accounting*. Pitman, Ch. 3.

A number of publications deal with service costing as applied to particular industries. The following are published by the Chartered Institute of Management Accountants, and are of recent date:

Jones, *Accounting in Local Government*. CIMA.
Meredith, *Accounting in the Water Industry*. CIMA.
Thornfield, *Accounting in Hotels*. CIMA.
Sloane, *Accounting in British Banking*. CIMA.

Chapter 11

Absorption and marginal costing

GETTING STARTED

Basic costing methods – such as have been discussed in the previous chapters – are devised to suit the methods by which goods are manufactured or services are provided. Superimposed onto these methods are principles and techniques which are devised to suit the *form in which it is decided to present information to management*. Two of these superimposed techniques are *absorption costing* and *marginal costing*.

Examination questions on this area of the syllabus are very popular with examiners, and with candidates. Unfortunately, many students fail to score as well as they might because of careless errors, or basic misunderstandings. Discussive questions tend to take the form of:

1. An explanation of terms and relationships.
2. Evaluations of the techniques, together with their inherent limitations.
3. The application of the methods to management decision-making.

Computational questions include:

1. The calculation of profits under absorption and marginal costing.
2. The calculation of break-even points, margins of safety, and differential profits.

Graphical questions also appear, seeking to test a knowledge of and an ability to apply simple graphs to particular situations.

ABSORPTION AND MARGINAL COSTING

Absorption and *marginal costing* are different methods of presenting costing information to management: the information so presented is the same information, deriving from the basic costing methods discussed earlier in this book. However, by presenting the information in different ways, various important aspects of that information can be emphasised in such a manner as to aid management decision-making.

The methods differ in the way in which they treat fixed costs:

Absorption costing assumes that fixed costs are related to products, so that in valuing closing stocks, both the fixed and the variable costs are included. In this way, some of Period I's fixed costs are carried over into Period II by way of the closing stock valuation.

Marginal costing assumes that fixed costs are related to time periods, such that Period I's fixed costs are set against Period I's income: the valuation of closing stocks, therefore, comprises only the variable costs. None of an earlier period's fixed costs appear in the accounts of a later period.

The following template indicates the nature of the respective calculations.

	Absorption costing			Marginal costing	
	(£)	(£)		(£)	(£)
Sales		XXX	Sales		XXX
Less: Variable costs	XXX		Less: Variable costs	XXX	
Fixed costs	XXX		Add opening stock	XXX	
	XXX			XXX	
Add opening stock	XXX		Less closing stock	XXX	
	XXX			XXX	
Less closing stock	XXX		Add fixed costs	XXX	
		XXX			XXX
Profit(Loss)		XXX			XXX

In each case, note the treatment of fixed costs: in absorption costing, the fixed costs are accounted for as part of the closing stock calculations: under marginal costing, the closing stock is calculated *before* the fixed costs are added.

Note that under the terms of SSAP 9, whilst either absorption or marginal costing approaches may be used for internal management purposes, absorption costing should be used for published financial accounts because costs and revenues should be matched in the period when the revenue arises, and not when the costs are incurred.

THE CONTRIBUTION

Central to the technique of marginal costing is the concept of the *contribution*. The contribution is the difference between the value of sales, and the variable costs of those sales. The contribution can be expressed either in absolute terms, or as a contribution per unit.

By definition, fixed costs remain unalterable over a given range of output; even at zero production, the fixed costs must be paid. Therefore, any income from sales which covers the marginal cost of production, and *contributes* something towards the burden of the fixed costs will improve the firm's position.

The relationship between sales, contribution and profit can be summarised:

$$\text{Total costs} = \text{Fixed costs} + \text{Variable costs}$$
$$\text{Contribution} = \text{Sales revenue} - \text{Variable costs}$$
$$\text{Profit} = \text{Contribution} - \text{Fixed costs}$$

Alternatively:

$$\text{Sales} - \text{Variable costs} = \text{Fixed costs} + \text{Profit}$$

The contribution/sales ratio

One of the most important ratios used in business is that which relates sales to the contribution. The ratio is calculated:

$$\frac{\text{Sales} - \text{Variable costs}}{\text{Sales}}$$

The (C/S) ratio may be expressed as a percentage merely by multiplying the above equation by '100'. The ratio measures the change in the contribution in relation to a change in sales.

USES OF MARGINAL COSTING

Marginal costing is used in the following situations:

1. Pricing decisions; where market prices move against a company, it will continue to produce a product as long as it can still cover the marginal costs of manufacturing that product.
2. Accept-reject decisions; where a company is offered the chance to fulfil a special order at a price below what it normally charges. Provided that the special price is above the marginal cost of manufacture, and that the firm has the productive capacity to fill the order, and that the special price will not affect existing markets, then the company can increase its profits by accepting the order.
3. Make-or-buy decisions; where a company must decide whether to manufacture a component or buy it in. Where the cost of buying in is less than the marginal cost of in-house manufacture, then it pays to purchase the product.

BREAK-EVEN ANALYSIS

Break-even analysis has to do with examining the relationship between revenue and fixed and variable costs at different levels of activity: that level of activity at which the company makes neither a profit nor a loss is termed the *break-even point*.

Break-even analysis can take the form of a series of simple equations, or of a simple graph. In either case, the following assumptions are made:

(a) that costs can be divided easily into fixed and variable costs;
(b) that the firm makes only one product – or that the product mix remains constant;
(c) that the company sells all that it makes: there are no opening or closing stocks;
(d) that there exists a linear relationship between sales and costs, i.e. that the relationship between sales and costs can be depicted on a graph by a series of straight lines.

The limitations of break-even analysis lie largely in the restrictions imposed by the above assumptions: costs may not be so easily classified into fixed and variable costs; firms do tend to make more than one product – and to vary their product mix; it is extremely unusual for companies to have no opening or closing stocks; some costs may be better illustrated by curved lines, or by 'kinked' lines.

The break-even output of a company can be found by the equation:

$$\text{Number of units to be sold to break even} = \frac{\text{Total fixed cost}}{\text{Contribution per unit}}$$

$$\text{Sales value at break-even point} = \frac{\text{Total fixed cost} \times \text{Sales value}}{\text{Total contribution}}$$

Alternatively:

$$\text{Sales value at break-even point} = \text{Number of units to be sold to break even} \times \text{Selling price/unit}$$

The linear cost function

In many problems connected with the behaviour of costs, accountants assume that the relationship between costs and output can be depicted on a graph using straight lines, indicating that as output increases, so too do costs. This assumption is sometimes called *the linear cost function*. The assumption is used in order to simplify problems, and to make them more easily resolvable. Because more complicated relationships are thus assumed away, the results of such simplified analyses must be used with caution.

Break-even charts

Break-even charts shown in Fig. 11.1 tend to take one of two forms. In version (a) candidates in examinations often confuse the total revenue and the total cost lines. Version (b) is less common, but it does have an advantage in emphasising that below the break-even point it is the fixed costs which are not being met. Whichever presentation is used, the break-even point occurs at the same level of output and revenue in any given situation.

When drawing charts, it is essential to label the axes, to label the lines on the chart, and to provide the chart with an explanatory title.

Fig. 11.1   Break-even charts

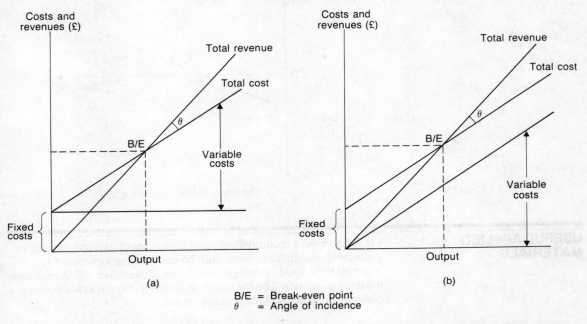

(a)

(b)

B/E = Break-even point
θ   = Angle of incidence

Margin of safety and angle of incidence

On break-even charts:

1. The *Margin of Safety* is the excess of normal or actual sales volume over the volume of sales at break-even point.
2. The *Angle of Incidence* is the angle at which the sales line cuts the total costs line. A large angle indicates that profits are being made at a high rate, and coupled with a high margin of safety indicates a favourable situation.

The contribution/sales graph

The contribution/sales graph is a form of break-even chart; it is sometimes called a *profit graph*. Fig. 11.2 shows profits/losses on the vertical axis, and the value of sales along the horizontal axis.

Fig. 11.2   Contribution/sales or profit graph

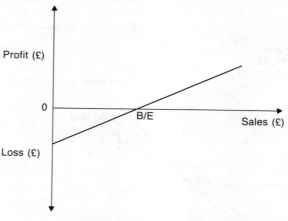

Contribution/sales or profit graph

**USEFUL APPLIED
MATERIALS**

Fig. 11.3 shows a monthly Profit and Loss account as it may appear in a marginal costing form. Note that the undertaking's overhead is assumed to be fixed, although some items of overhead will change with the level of activity. The contribution is clearly shown, as is a running comparison of actual with planned figures.

*Fig. 11.3   Monthly Profit and Loss Account
Statement in Marginal Costing Form*

Line		Actual £	Budget £	Gain + Loss − £
1.	Sales - budgeted		50,000	
	– actual	40,000		−10,000
2.	Income from goods sold		40,000	
3.	*Less* variable cost of goods sold:			
4.	Purchases of direct material	20,100		
5.	Direct labour	6,000		
6.	Sales carriage	400		
7.	Stock increase (−) or decrease (+)	+2,000		
8.	Total variable cost of goods sold	28,500	28,000	−500
9.	**Gross profit (or contribution)**	11,500	12,000	−500
10.	**Less fixed overhead:**			
11.	Salaries	1,100	1,000	−100
12.	Indirect labour	2,500	2,300	−200
13.	Overtime premium	300	250	−50
14.	National insurance	250	270	+20
15.	Pensions	300	300	
16.	Consumable stores	400	430	+30
17.	Tools	500	510	+10
18.	Electricity	700	750	+50
19.	Water	100	105	+5
20.	Fuel	150	165	+15
21.	Motor car expenses, petrol and oil	200	250	+50
22.	Maintenance	650	615	−35
23.	Rent and rates	300	300	
24.	Insurance	80	78	−2
25.	Depreciation	700	700	
26.	Advertising	600	300	−300
27.	Travel expenses	200	150	−50
28.	Printing and stationery	90	100	+10
29.	Postages	70	60	−10
30.	Telephones and telegrams	60	50	−10
31.	Legal and professional charges	50	50	
32.	**Total fixed overhead**	9,300	8,733	−567
33.	**Profit before taxation**	2,200	3,267	−1,067

(Source: Rickwood and Piper, Marginal Costing, CIMA)

RECENT EXAMINATION QUESTIONS

Question **1** tests knowledge of the terms absorption and marginal costing, and contribution. Question **2** tests an understanding of the meaning of fixed and variable costs. Question **3** requires the application of graphs to particular situations. Question **4** seeks an explanation of cost behaviour, and **5** looks at the limitations of break-even analysis. Question **6** demands the preparation of accounts under both marginal and absorption costing, and it has been selected for the *Tutor's Answer*. Question **7** applies marginal costing to a make-or-buy decision. Questions **8** and **9** require the calculation of break-even points.

1

(a) Define the terms:

      (i) Absorption costing;

      (ii) Marginal costing;

      (iii) Contribution.

(5 marks)

(b) Explain why absorption costing may give incorrect or misleading results when changes in levels of productive activity occur.

(3 marks)

(c) Marginal costing is frequently used to assist management in making decisions. Indicate THREE areas of decision making in which marginal costing can be particularly useful.

(7 marks)

(d) Show, preferably in the form of an equation, the relationships that exist among sales, profit, costs, and contribution, and indicate how this knowledge may be used by management.

(3 marks)

(RSA Stage III, April 1986)

2 Explain whether you agree with each of the following statements:

      (i) All direct costs are variable.

      (ii) Variable costs are controllable and fixed costs are not.

      (iii) Sunk costs are irrelevant when providing decision making information.

(9 marks)

(ACCA Level 1, December 1984)

3 The graphs shown in Fig. 11.4 reflect the pattern of certain overhead cost items in a manufacturing company in a year. The vertical axes of the graphs represent for each item the total cost incurred. The horizontal axes represent the volume of production. The zero point of the cost and volume is at the intersection of the two axes.

(i) Identify in each case which graph represents the cost behaviour of the overhead cost items given below; and

(ii) Give a brief explanation of your choices.

1. Cost of a service   £1 per unit produced with a maximum charge of £3,000 per annum.

2. Rent of a factory   £10,000 per annum.

3. Supervision salaries   One charge-hand for every ten direct
                           workers or less, and one foreman for
                           every three charge-hands. For a week of
                           40 hours this represents:

                           Under 400 hours, one charge-hand;
                           401–800 hours, two charge-hands;
                           801–1,200 hours, three charge-hands and
                           one foreman.

4. Depreciation   Charged to a cost centre on a cost per unit
                           basis.

5. Maintenance   An annual charge of £2,000 and a charge of
                           £2 each for units produced, with a
                           maximum charge of £5,000 per annum.

Fig. 11.4

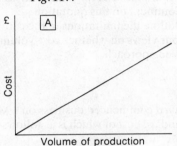

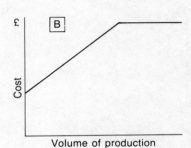

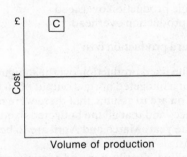

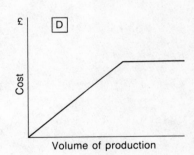

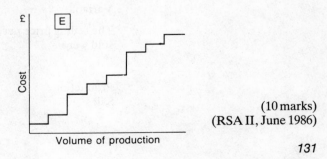

(10 marks)
(RSA II, June 1986)

4

It is commonly agreed that cost behaviour is much more complex than is allowed for in the conventional cost accounting model, and that costs cannot always be divided into fixed or variable categories.

Describe some alternative forms of cost behaviour that may be relevant for the management accountant. Consider the extent to which cost accounting systems are based on the linear cost function assumption, and discuss the proposition that such an assumption can be a serious defect.

(17 marks)
(ACCA Level 2, June 1985)

5

(a) 'Cost-volume-profit analysis should not be restricted by the limitations of break-even analysis and the break-even chart.' Comment on this quotation.

Outline the limitations of the conventional break-even chart and give your views on whether cost-volume-profit analysis can provide an improved approach.

(9 marks)
(ACCA Level 2, June 1984)

6

X Limited commenced business on 1 March making one product only, the standard cost of which is as follows:

	(£)
Direct labour	5
Direct material	8
Variable production overhead	2
Fixed production overhead	5
Standard production cost	20

The fixed production overhead figure has been calculated on the basis of a budgeted normal output of 36,000 units per annum.

You are to assume that there were no expenditure or efficiency variances and that all the budgeted fixed expenses are incurred evenly over the year. March and April are to be taken as equal period months.

Selling, distribution and administration expenses are:

Fixed	£120,000 per annum
Variable	15% of the sales value

The selling price per unit is £35 and the number of units produced and sold were:

	March	April
Production	2,000	3,200
Sales	1,500	3,000

(a) Prepare profit statements for each of the months of March and April, using:

    (i)   marginal costing, and
    (ii) absorption costing

(15 marks)

(b) Present a reconciliation of the profit or loss figures given in your answers to (a)(i) and (a)(ii), accompanied by a brief explanation.

(5 marks)

(c) Comment briefly upon which costing principle, i.e. marginal or absorption, should be used for what purpose(s) and why, referring to any statutory or other mandatory constraints.

(5 marks)

(CIMA Stage 2 Specimen)

7

The management of an engineering company manufacturing a range of products is considering next year's production, purchase and sales budgets. Shown below are the budgeted total unit costs for two of the components and two of the products manufactured by the company.

	Component		Product	
	12 £/unit	14 £/unit	VW £/unit	XY £/unit
Direct material	18	26	12	28
Direct labour	16	4	12	24
Variable overhead	8	2	6	12
Fixed overhead	20	5	15	30
	62	37	45	94

Components 12 and 14 are incorporated into other products manufactured and sold by the company, but not the two products shown above. It is possible to purchase Components 12 and 14 from another company for £60 per unit and £30 per unit respectively.

The anticipated selling prices of products VW and XY are £33 and £85 respectively.

(a) Advise the management of the company whether it would be profitable to:
    (i)   purchase either of the above components;
    (ii) sell either of the above products.

(4 marks)

(b) State clearly, and where appropriate comment upon, the assumptions you have made in answering (a) above.

(9 marks)

(c) Consider how the following additional information would affect your advice in (a) above.

(i) Next year's budgeted production requirements for the two components are 7,000 units of Component 12 and 6,000 units of Component 14. Next year's budgeted sales for the two products are Product VW 5,000 units, and Product XY 4,000 units.

(ii) A special machine is used exclusively by the above two components and two products, and for technical reasons the machine can only be allowed to operate for 80,000 machine hours next year.

The budgeted usage of the machine is:

Component 12: 8 machine hours   Product VW: 6 machine hours

Component 14: 2 machine hours   Product XY: 12 machine hours

The operating costs of the machine have been included in the unit costs shown in (a) above.

(9 marks)

(ACCA Level 1, June 1985)

8

David Alaeze makes a product called 'Aler-eze', a highly effective medicine for hay fever sufferers. Aler-eze sells for £2.40 per pack. The variable cost of manufacturing a pack is £1.40. Mr Alaeze has a factory fixed overhead that costs £50,000 p.a. The factory capacity is limited to 200,000 packs of 'Aler-eze'. The factory runs at 100% capacity and sells all its products.

However, by a change of processing and formula, David Alaeze could increase the factory capacity to 500,000 packs p.a. These could all be sold if the selling price drops by 25 per cent and sold in a new package with a new marketing strategy. This introduction will require an increase in the fixed overhead by £15,000 p.a., but the variable cost will decrease by 40p a pack.

(i) Conduct a break-even analysis based on this information;
(ii) Show the break-even point, the profit and the margin of safety for both the existing and the proposed production.

(20 marks)

(ACEA, Part II, December 1985)

9

Formula L14 is a chemical product, manufactured and marketed by Durham Chemicals plc. It is planned to sell 80,000 tonnes of L14 in the three month period commencing July 1986, at a price of £20 per tonne. Fixed overhead is budgeted at £275,000 for the period, and the expected net profit is £165,000.

Using either graphical or arithmetical procedure, ascertain:

(i)   The total contribution;

(3 marks)

(ii) The contribution/sales ratio;

(3 marks)

(iii) The contribution per tonne;

(3 marks)

(iv) The extra profit arising from selling a further 1,250 tonnes;

(5 marks)

(v)   The additional sales required to produce the same profit as that shown in the present budget (£165,000) if the selling price is reduced to £18.50.

(6 marks)

(LCC Higher, Summer 1986)

OUTLINE ANSWERS

1

(a) (i) *Absorption costing*: a principle whereby fixed as well as variable costs are allotted to cost units, and total overheads are absorbed according to activity level. The term may be used where production costs only are allotted, or where the costs of all functions are so allotted.

(ii) *Marginal costing*: a principle whereby variable costs are charged to cost units and the fixed cost attributable to the relevant period is written off in full against the *contribution* for that period.

(iii) *The contribution*: the difference between sales value and the variable cost of those sales, expressed either in absolute terms or as a contribution per unit.

(b) Absorption costing includes fixed costs in the valuation of closing stocks of work-in-progress and finished goods. When changes in output occur, stocks are likely to fluctuate, too, so that *different* amounts of fixed costs are carried forward into future periods, with a consequent affect upon recorded profits.

(c) Marginal costing is often used in:

(i) pricing decisions: in the short-term provided that prices are equal to or above the marginal cost, the company should continue to produce the item.

(ii) accept-reject decisions concerning special orders: when deciding whether to undertake work over and above normal output, the revenue from the special order should be at least equal to its marginal cost.

(iii) make-or-buy decisions: a company should buy-in those items whose marginal cost of manufacture are greater than the buying-in price.

(d) Total cost   = Fixed costs + Variable costs
     Contribution = Sales revenue − Variable costs
     Profit   = Contribution − Fixed costs

2

Not all direct costs are variable: direct costs are those which can readily be traced to a particular cost centre: whether these easily traceable costs vary with output is another matter. The production manager's salary may be easily traced to a particular department, but may not vary with production.

It is not possible to generalise over whether classes of cost are controllable; the terms *fixed* and *variable* refer to the behaviour of a cost over a defined time period: the terms have no bearing upon a cost's control. All costs are controllable by someone within the organisation if sufficient time and effort are expended.

Sunk costs refer to assets which can continue to serve their present purpose, but which have no significant resaleable value for another purpose. Once money is spent on them, it cannot be retrieved. In this sense, therefore, the statement is true: a sunk cost is one which has already taken place, and cannot be affected by current decisions.

3

1.	Cost of a service	Graph D:	shows costs rising as output increases, up to a maximum of £3,000.
2.	Rent of factory	Graph C:	£10,000 rent has to be paid irrespective of level of output.
3.	Supervision salaries	Graph E:	shows stepped costs, increasing at 400-hour intervals, with larger steps every 1,200 hours.
4.	Depreciation	Graph A:	charged on a cost per unit basis: increases in proportion to output.
5.	Maintenance	Graph B:	annual fixed charge which must be met even at zero output, plus £2 for each unit produced, with a maximum of £5,000 per annum.

4

A *model* is a representation of the real world. The cost accountant tends to represent the real world of costs by means of a straight line. This is what is meant by the term the *linear cost function*.

See as examples the graphs used in Fig. 11.5. Insofar as stepped costs are recognised (A), they are merely variations on the linear theme, and they tend to be divided into fixed and variable elements. If the range of activity being examined is small enough, (B), then the linear assumption may well serve to represent costs which show a

Fig. 11.5 Graphs of cost.

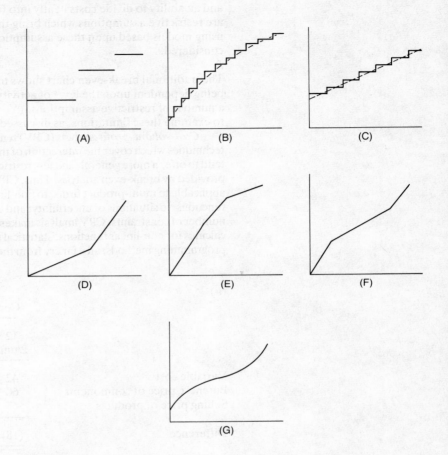

Graphs of cost

curvilinear feature, i.e. costs which can be represented by curved lines upon a graph. If the steps are small and regular, it may still be possible to show them as a straight line (C).

The conventional view also assumes that variable costs remain constant; and whilst this may be true over particular ranges of activity, it may not be true over all levels of output. *Kinked* schedules may be apparent in some circumstances (D, E, F).

Some costs may be *curvilinear*; they may appear on a graph as curves. This is especially true where increasing or decreasing returns to scale are available (G).

Note, too, that the level of output is not the only factor likely to influence costs.

The basic cost accounting assumptions of linear cost functions, and an ability to divide costs neatly into fixed and variable categories are restrictive assumptions which bring their own limitations. When using models based upon these assumptions, the limitations must be considered.

5

The traditional break-even chart shows total cost and total revenue as being dependent upon the level of activity. The analysis is based upon a number of restrictive assumptions. (Your answer should then go on to examine these limitations, as discussed in the text above, p. 126.)

Cost-volume-profit analysis (CPV) tends to refer to a number of techniques which cover the interaction of the three variables, and which tend to offer a more general, and less restrictive, analysis than that provided by break-even analysis. Thus, CPV analysis can be made applicable to multi-product firms; to non-linear cost and revenue functions; to situations of uncertainty; and to situations containing a number of constraints. CPV analysis makes use of matrix methods, of calculus for non-linear functions, statistical techniques, and mathematical programming methods: all a far cry from the traditional break-even chart.

7

(a)

	Component		Product	
	12 £/unit	14 £/unit	VW £/unit	XY £/unit
Variable cost	42	32	30	64
Purchase price of components	60	30		
Selling price of products			33	85
Difference	(18)	2	(3)	(21)

Advise management to produce Component 12 because variable cost is lower than purchase price; but buy in Component 14 because it can be purchased marginally cheaper than the firm can make it.

The variable costs of both products are lower than the selling prices, and so advise that both products be made.

(b) Assumptions made: prime costs and variable overheads vary directly with number of units made and sold; additional costs will not be incurred as a result of purchasing Component 14; production of any components or products will not affect the fixed overheads incurred by the company; limited resources will not restrict the production required; profitability is being measured in terms of absolute amounts of contribution; and budgeted variable cost and selling prices are accurate.

(c) The additional information gives rise to the following. Note that Component 14 has been ignored, because our advice in (a) was that this should be bought in.

	(i) Production required (units)	(ii) Machine time per unit (hours)	(iii) Machine hours required [(i) × (iii)]
Component 12	7,000	8	56,000
Product VW	5,000	6	30,000
Product XY	4,000	12	48,000
Total machine hours			134,000
Total hours available			80,000
Shortfall			54,000

Because there is insufficient machine time to produce all the company plans, it is necessary to rank the products according to their profitability in relation to the machine time:

	Component 12	Product VW	XY
Purchase price (£/unit)	60		
Selling price (£/unit)		33	85
Variable manufacturing cost (£/unit)	42	30	64
Contribution saved/earned (£/unit)	18	3	21
Special machine hours used	8	6	12
Contribution/machine hour (£)	2.25	0.50	1.75
Ranking	(1)	(3)	(2)

As a result of the above, suggest produce all of Component 12 (7,000 units requiring 56,000 machine hours) and spend the remaining 24,000 hours on Product XY. At 12 hours per unit, this will enable 2,000 units of XY to be produced.

8
(i)

	Existing product		Proposed product
Sales revenue (£/unit)	2.40	(£2.40 × 75%)	1.80
Variable cost (£/unit)	1.40	(£1.40 − £0.40)	1.00
Contribution (£/unit)	1.00		0.80
Fixed cost (£ total)	50,000	(£50,000 + £15,000)	65,000
Break-even point (units)	50,000		81,250
Total output (units)	200,000		500,000
Profit (£ total)	150,000		335,000
Margin of safety (units)	150,000		418,750

Once the fixed costs have been covered, the contribution accrues as profit. Thus, with the existing product, the first 50,000 units are needed to break-even; thereafter, the contribution accruing from the remainder of output (200,000–50,000 = 150,000) gives rise to profits of 150,000 × £1.0 = £150,000.

With the proposed product, 81,250 items are needed to break-even. The balance of production (500,000 − 81,250 = 418,750) contributes towards profit: 418,750 × £0.80 = £335,000.

The margin of safety is the difference between actual output, and that output necessary to reach break-even point.

(ii)   *Fig. 11.6 Break-even charts*
       (Note: Charts are drawn to different scales)

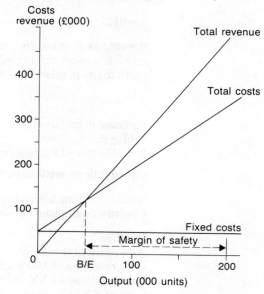

(a) Existing production

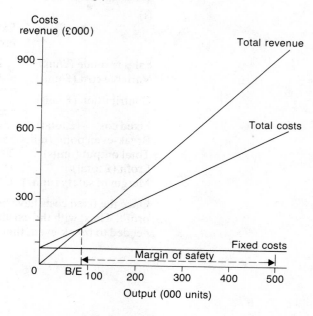

(b) Proposed production

9

(i)

	Per tonne (£)	(£)	Total (£000)	(£000)
Sales		20.00		1,600
Fixed overheads	3.4375		275	
Profit	2.0625		165	
Contribution		5.50		440
Variable costs		14.50		1,160

The total contribution is £440,000.

(ii) The contribution/sales ratio:

$$\frac{\text{Sales} - \text{Variable costs}}{\text{Sales}}$$

$$= \frac{£1,600 - £1,160}{£1,600} = 0.275$$

(iii) The contribution per tonne is £5.50.

(iv) An additional 1,250 tonnes sold, assuming there is no increase in fixed costs would increase profits by the total amount of the contribution;

$$1,250 \times £5.50 = £6,875$$

(v) a reduction in the selling price which leaves all other variables unchanged will result in a reduction in the contribution: £20 − £18.50 = £1.50. The new contribution will therefore be: £5.50 − £1.50 = £4.00.

In order to earn the same profit, sales will need to be: £440,000 ÷ £4.00 = 110,000 tonnes:

	(£000)	(£000)
Sales 110,000 × £18.50	2,035	
Less variable costs (£14.50 × 110,000)	1,595	
		440
Less fixed costs		275
Desired profit		165

A TUTOR'S ANSWER

You do not need an understanding of budgeting or standard costing to answer this question: the question merely tests your knowledge of absorption and marginal costing. When scanning your examination paper, therefore, do study the questions carefully to see just what is involved, otherwise you may ignore a question which you can do well, or conversely, begin a question which will present you with difficulties.

6

(a) (i)

Marginal costing

	March (£)	March (£)	April (£)	April (£)
Sales: 1,500 × £35		52,500		
3,000 × £35				105,000
Less: Variable cost of sales				
Opening stock (April)			7,500	
Variable manufacturing cost;				
2,000 × £15	30,000			
3,200 × £15			48,000	
			55,500	
Less closing stock: 500 × £15	7,500			
700 × £15			10,500	
	22,500		45,000	
Variable distribution &c				
(15% sales)	7,875		15,750	
		30,375		60,750
Contribution		22,125		44,250
Less: Fixed costs: Production	15,000		15,000	
Selling &c	10,000		10,000	
		25,000		25,000
Profit (Loss)		(2,875)		19,250

142

	March (£)	(£)	April (£)	(£)
Sales: 1,500 × £35		52,500		
3,000 × £35				105,000
Less: Cost of sales:				
Opening stock (April)		10,000		
Production cost: 2,000 × £20	40,000			
3,200 × £20			64,000	
			74,000	
Less closing stock: 500 × £20	10,000			
700 × £20			14,000	
	30,000		60,000	
Fixed production overhead: (1)				
underabsorbed	5,000			
overabsorbed			(1,000)	
Production cost of sales		35,000		59,000
Gross profit		17,500		46,000
Less: Variable selling &c:				
15% sales	7,875		15,750	
Fixed selling &c	10,000		10,000	
		17,875		25,750
Profit (Loss)		(375)		20,250

Note (1): The question tells us that the fixed production overhead figure of £5 per unit had been calculated on the basis of a budgeted normal output of 36,000 units per annum. Since we are told that March and April are equal period months, we can assume that the monthly budgeted output = 36,000 ÷ 12 = 3,000.

During March, production was only 2,000 units; the *underabsorbed* fixed overhead was therefore (3,000 − 2,000) × £5 = £5,000. During April, output was 3,200 units; the *overabsorbed* overhead was therefore (3,200 − 3,000) × £5 = £1,000.

(b)

Reconciliation of profit

	March (£)	April (£)
Marginal approach: Profit (Loss)	(2,875)	19,250
Fixed production overhead c/fwd in March's closing stock: 500 × £5	2,500	(2,500)
Fixed production overhead c/fwd in April's closing stock: 700 × £5		3,500
Absorption approach: Profit (Loss)	(375)	20,250

(c) Managers often prefer to adopt the marginal approach to aid control and decision-making; but SSAP 9 favours the absorption approach when valuing stocks for balance sheet purposes, since fixed overheads are included in stock valuations under the absorption method.

A STEP FURTHER

Arnold and Hope, *Accounting for Management Decisions*. Prentice Hall, Chs 1 and 3.
Daff, *Cost and Management Accounting*. Woodhead Faulkner, Ch. 6.
Harvey and Nettleton, *Management Accounting*. Mitchell Beazley, Chs 3 and 4.
Lucey, *Costing*. D. P. Publications, Chs 18–21.
Lucey, *Management Accounting*. D. P. Publications, Chs 14–16.
Norkett, *Management Accounting*. Pitman, Ch. 6.
Riddle, *Stage I Cost Accounting*. Northwick, Chs 5 and 6.

Chapter 12

Budgeting and budgetary control

GETTING STARTED

Examination questions on these topics are very popular with examiners at all levels, since it is in the area of budgeting and budgetary control that costing methods begin to contribute towards the management processes of planning and control.

Discussive questions include:

1. The definition of terms, and the comparison of concepts which lie behind the terms.
2. A description of the procedures to be followed when introducing systems involving budgets and budgetary control.
3. The value of the techniques as aids to the management process.

Computational questions tend to comprise the construction of:

1. Operating budgets – for production and for cash.
2. A master budget from information supplied.
3. Flexible budgets, for different levels of activity.

ESSENTIAL PRINCIPLES

A *budget* is a plan expressed in terms of money. It is prepared in advance of the period to which it refers. It usually shows planned income to be earned, planned expenditure to be incurred, and the planned capital to be employed to achieve stated objectives.

A budget is prepared for a given period of time – usually a year – and this time is referred to as the *budget period*.

Budgetary control is the setting of budgets which relate the responsibilities of individual managers to the needs of an agreed set of policies. Budgetary control demands a continuous comparison of actual with planned results, and implies that necessary action will be taken to influence activities if actual performance differs from planned performance.

OPERATING AND CAPITAL BUDGETS

Operating budgets – sometimes called departmental or functional budgets – are income or expenditure plans relating to a particular department or function. The function may be a department or a process.

Operating budgets include:

marketing cost budget   production cost budget
personnel budget   purchasing budget
research and development budget

Capital budgets have to do with the long-term provision of resources, and include fixed assets, working capital, loan capital, and long-term cash budgets. The subjects of capital budgets, and capital budgeting are discussed in Chapter 14.

THE LIMITING FACTOR

The *limiting factor* (sometimes called the *key factor*) is that influence which at any time limits the activity of a business. Note that a business's limiting factor may change from time to time. At one moment it may be a limit upon how much the business can sell; at another, it may be a restriction upon its level of output – brought about by raw material shortages, or a shortage of capital equipment or a lack of skilled labour.

A further name for the limiting factor is the *principal budget factor*, indicating the particular influence upon activity which must be taken into account when budgets are being prepared.

BUDGET PREPARATION

The responsibility for the preparation of a company's budget is usually that of senior management. Often, a budget committee will be established comprising senior managers from the various departments. The committee will draft the general approach to be used in preparing the budget, and will appoint one of the organisation's senior accountants to act as the budget manager.

The budget manager will:

- Issue instructions to all departments detailing how the budgets are to be prepared, and establishing the deadlines to be met.
- Offer historical and other information to the operating managers to help them in the preparation of their budgets.
- Help the managers with any difficulties they may have in preparing the budgets.
- Receive and check the budgets from the department.
- Submit the departmental budgets to the budget committee for agreement.
- Prepare the company's master budget from the departmental budgets.

The *master budget* is a summary of all the operating budgets, and it usually takes the form of a set of budget final accounts.

The operating budgets will be prepared by working back from the limiting factor. Thus, if sales constitute the limiting factor, then the sales budgets will be derived first, and then the production budget next (Fig. 12.1).

Fig. 12.1   The budgeting sequence

Where production is the limiting factor, the level of sales will be determined by output, as will the materials, and labour budgets.

THE SALES BUDGET

Two approaches are usually used in combination:

1. A statistical forecast based upon the likely effects of the general economic climate upon the firm's markets;
2. An introspective consideration of the likely market developments based upon the views of the firm's own sales force.

THE PRODUCTION BUDGET

Where sales is the limiting factor, the production budget will derive from it. The production budget can be expressed either in terms of units to be produced, or in monetary terms: often, it is expressed in both forms.

When drafting the production budget, a decision will be needed concerning stock levels. If output increases in advance of sales, stocks of finished items will increase: if sales outpace production, then the firm will need to draw upon stocks to make good the deficiency. With raw material stocks, too, any planned increase in output will demand the purchasing of additional materials to support that output.

Wherever possible, companies – and their work force – prefer to maintain even production levels, allowing stocks to rise and fall to equalise the rates of sales and production. Steady production levels make for regular working hours, and enable maintenance to be planned.

CASH BUDGETS

Cash budgets include a company's cash and bank balances. Cash budgets fulfil three functions:

1. They help to ensure that sufficient cash is available when needed.
2. They show up any future cash shortages that are likely to arise, enabling action to be taken in advance to ensure adequate funding.
3. They show up any future cash surpluses, which can then be loaned or invested.

Cash budgets show the interaction between two schedules: the receipts schedule, and the payments schedule. The receipts schedule is a list of expected receipts broken down month by month. The payments schedule is the planned monthly expenditure. When the total of planned monthly receipts is added to the planned opening cash balance – and when total planned monthly expenditures are deducted – then the planned closing balance for the month is shown.

The template for a cash budget is shown below:

Cash budget (£000)
for
the six months ending 30 June, 19 ——

	J	F	M	A	M	J
Opening balance	XX	XX	XX	XX	XX	XX
Add receipts	XX	XX	XX	XX	XX	XX
	XX	XX	XX	XX	XX	XX
Less payments	XX	XX	XX	XX	XX	XX
Closing balance	XX	XX	XX	XX	XX	XX

Note that the closing balance for January becomes the opening balance for February, etc. See, too, how the layout of the cash budget lends itself to computerised spreadsheet application.

Sometimes, the two schedules are incorporated into the cash budget itself, so that within the body of the cash budget the monthly receipts are listed and added to the opening balance; and the monthly payments are listed, and are deducted.

FLEXIBLE BUDGETS

A *flexible budget* is designed to change with fluctuations in output, turnover, or other variable factors. In doing this it recognises the difference in behaviour between fixed and variable costs in relation to such fluctuations.

If senior management decide to increase output beyond what was originally planned, it would clearly be unfair to apply the previously agreed level of planned expenditure to the production manager's performance. A flexible budget provides planned expenditure for different levels of activity, and in this way endeavours to overcome such inequities.

ZERO BASE BUDGETING

Zero base budgeting is a method of budgeting whereby all activities are re-evaluated each time a budget is prepared. Each budget begins with the assumption that the activity does not exist, and is at zero cost. Every item of budgeted expenditure is then examined carefully in order to justify its inclusion in the budget itself.

The approach is generally applicable to budgets which comprise large elements of overhead costs; and is often seen as particularly appropriate to the public sector.

Fig. 12.2 is taken from the accounts of Cambridgeshire County Council for the year 1985–86. Each committee's gross revenue spending is shown, together with the effects of income earned, and the revised budget for the year. Variations between budgeted figures and actual spending are shown, together with net spending for the previous year. Underpinning each of the committee totals will be a more detailed budget broken down by type of expense and income. Many county councils publish such detailed accounts, and these are usually freely available on request.

Fig. 12.2

Committee	Gross Spending 1985–86	Income 1985–86	Net Spending 1985–86	Revised Budget 1985–86	Variation 1985–86	Net Spending 1984–85
	£000	£000	£000	£000	£000	£000
Education	174,148	27,718	146,430	146,711	− 281	137,522
Social Services	30,906	6,944	23,962	23,817	+ 145	21,262
Transportation	27,152	6,132	21,020	22,089	− 1,069	19,300
Police	30,202	16,785	13,417	13,015	+ 402	12,472
Public Protection	8,492	805	7,687	7,546	+ 141	7,201
Libraries and Museums	4,637	282	4,355	4,417	− 62	4,102
Property	2,271	4,195	(1,924)	(1,848)	− 76	(1,611)
Policy	7,713	10,334	(2,621)	(588)	− 2,033	(1,601)
Magistrates' Courts	1,868	1,503	365	364	+ 1	346
Probation	1,649	1,340	309	331	− 22	327
Total Committee Spending	289,038	76,038	213,000	215,854	− 2,854	199,320
Other Movements			(6,226)			(4,686)
Total Net Spending			206,774			194,634
Paid for by: Rate Income			134,196			126,213
Rate Support Grant – Block Grant			74,199			78,377
Contribution from (to) Balances			(1,621)			(9,956)
Total Income			206,774			194,634

Source: Cambridgeshire County Council

Questions **1, 2, 3, 5,** and **6** seek to test an understanding of terms and concepts. Questions **2, 3,** and **4** examine a knowledge of the budget-setting procedures to be followed. Question **7** looks at the compilation of a cash budget, and question **8** is an example of a simple master budget. Question **7** has been chosen for the *Tutor's Answer*.

1   What do you understand by the terms 'budgets', 'budgeting', and 'budgetary control'?
What are the purposes of budgets? Briefly state the main and secondary uses of budgets.

(20 marks)
(ACEA Part II, June 1986)

2
(a)   'A budget is a forecast.'
           'A budget is a target.'
           'A budget is an allocation of resources.'
           'A budget is a measuring rod.'

Discuss any conflicts that are inherent in the above views of budgets. Discuss the general validity of each of the statements and give your own views on the nature of budgets.

(8 marks)

(b)   Discuss the problems that are likely to be involved in setting and agreeing the budget for an organisation's Research and Development Department and in instituting a system of financial control for such a department.

(9 marks)
(ACCA Level 2, December 1984)

3   A small engineering company, manufacturing a range of ten different components for the car industry, is unable to meet the full demand because of a 'limiting factor'.

(i)   State briefly what you understand by the term 'limiting factor' and give three examples other than sales.

(10 marks)

(ii)   In the circumstances outlined above, enumerate and explain what steps should be taken by the management to plan production of components.

(10 marks)
(LCC Higher, Spring, 1986)

4   The technique of budgetary control is being introduced in a manufacturing company.

(i)   List six executives you would expect to be members of the budget committee which is being set up under the chairmanship of the managing director.

(6 marks)

(ii) State briefly what you consider will be the main advantage derived from the establishment of the committee.

(10 marks)

(iii) List what you consider to be the four most important duties of the budget committee.

(4 marks)

(LCC Higher, Spring 1985)

Note: this paper did not show the marks allocated to questions: the marks shown are those thought likely to have been given.

5 Exe plc has appointed a new chairman who will soon be involved in a board meeting at which budgets for the next financial year will be appraised. He is concerned with recent reports that managers are claiming that they have no control over a number of items in their budgets, so are losing interest in their performance assessments.

You are required, as management accountant, to write a report to the Chairman to explain and discuss the following:

(a) The objectives of a system of budgetary control;

(10 marks)

(b) Some of the concepts or principles of a modern system of budgetary control which could be introduced to alleviate the situation as represented by the managers.

(10 marks)

(CIMA Professional Stage, May 1986)

6 Many people believe that the benefits of budgetary control are limited to the private sector and that the only way to make any meaningful contribution to the public sector is by the application of the 'zero-based' budgeting technique.

You are required to describe the theory behind the technique and to show how it would be implemented. Suggest the benefits that may accrue from such introduction.

(20 marks)

(ACEA, Part II December 1984)

7

(a) The following information relates to XY Ltd:

Month	Wages incurred £000	Material purchases £000	Overhead £000	Sales £000
February	6	20	10	30
March	8	30	12	40
April	10	25	16	60
May	9	35	14	50
June	12	30	18	70
July	10	25	16	60
August	9	25	14	50
September	9	30	14	50

(i)   It is expected that the cash balance on 31 May will be £22,000.

(ii) The wages may be assumed to be paid within the month they are incurred.

(iii) It is company policy to pay creditors for materials three months after receipt.

(iv) Debtors are expected to pay two months after delivery.

(v)   Included in the overhead figures is £2,000 per month which represents depreciation on two cars and one delivery van.

(vi) There is a one-month delay in paying the overhead expenses.

(vii) Ten per cent of the monthly sales are for cash and 90 per cent are sold on credit.

(viii)A commission of 5 per cent is paid to agents on all the sales on credit, but this is not paid until the month following the sales to which it relates; this expense is *not* included in the overhead figures shown.

(ix) It is intended to repay a loan of £25,000 on 30 June.

(x)   Delivery is expected in July of a new machine costing £45,000, of which £15,000 will be paid on delivery and £15,000 in each of the following two months.

(xi) Assume that the overdraft facilities are available if required.

You are required to prepare a cash budget for each of the three months of June, July and August.

(14 marks)

(b) 'Experts stress that one of the most vital uses of management accounts is regularly to monitor cash flow – moneys coming into the company each month minus the moneys going out.'
(*Financial Times* – 8 March, 1983.)

You are required to comment on the above statement and include in your answer the chief benefits obtained from the preparation of cash budgets.

(6 marks)
(CIMA Foundation, May 1985)

8 Sales for the current financial year, which ends on 31 May, are expected to amount to £1,680,000, whilst cost totals are expected to be as follows:

	Variable £000	Fixed £000
Direct materials	500	
Direct wages	360	
Production overhead	120	220
General administration		100
Marketing (including advertising)	84	166

In preparing the budget for the year commencing 1 June next, the following changes have to be allowed for:

		June	July	Aug
Receipts Schedule				
Sales	-2	54	45	63
Cash	Ø	7	6	5
		61	51	68

		June	July	Aug
Payments Schedule		June	July	Aug
Wages	Ø	12	10	9
Materials	-3	30	25	35
Commission ~~Overheads~~	+1	2.25	3 3.15	2.7
Overheads	+1	12	16	14
Loan		25		
New Machine			15	15
		81.25	69.15	75.7

Cash Budgets	June	July	Aug
Opening Balance	22,~~000~~	1.75	
Add receipts	61,~~000~~	69.15	
	83,~~000~~	70.90	
Less payments	81.25 ~~81.25~~		
	1.75 ~~75~~		

(i)   production and sales volume to be increased by 25 per cent;
(ii) prices of direct materials to rise by 8 per cent;
(iii) hourly wage rates to be increased by 10 per cent;
(iv) selling prices to be increased by 2½ per cent;
(v)   factory management salaries to be increased by £15,000 and office salaries by a similar amount;
(vi) expenditure on advertising to be increased by £35,000.

Prepare the budget for the year commencing 1 June next.

(20 marks)

(LCC Intermediate, May 1985)

OUTLINE ANSWERS

1 Your answer should define each of the three terms clearly, and should show how they are interrelated. You should also set the activities of budgeting and budgetary control in their managerial context by discussing the purpose of budgets in relation to the activities of planning, motivating, and control.

2

(a)   To regard budgets as a *forecast* emphasises their predictive function – as with cash budgets, which aim to show the pattern of receipts and payments that is *thought* will occur.

The view that budgets are *targets* stresses the motivational aspects upon managers, in their efforts to increase income or to reduce costs.

Where budgets are used to *allocate scarce resources* amongst competing departments or sections, some method will be needed to ensure that the planned expenditure targets are not exceeded. Thus, *cash limits* may be applied, such that departments will be prevented from spending above an agreed total.

The view that a budget is a *measuring rod*, identifies the opportunities that budgets offer for comparing actual with planned activities. *Standard costing* takes this feature a stage further.

(b)   Research and Development departments represent one of the most difficult of departments for budgeting purposes, since much of the work is irregular in nature, and carries a high degree of uncertainty. Often, the R&D budget is fixed on the basis of previous years' expenditure; and since many of the expenses are by way of fixed costs this may be quite acceptable. Sometimes, R&D budgets are set by using a formula relating R&D expenditure to sales or to income; but such formulae do not remove the innate difficulties – they merely offer a basis for further discussion.

3

(i)   Define *limiting factor* carefully, and give examples drawn from productive capacity, availability of raw materials, storage capability, finance, managerial limit.

(ii) In preparing a budget, work from the limiting factor. Thus, if productive capacity is the limiting factor, this will determine the

153

quantity – and possibly the timing – of raw material purchases, and the quantity and type of labour needed. It will also determine total sales. The availability of raw materials will determine the level of output (and thus the level of sales) and the labour needed. Finance will determine the overall scale of operations – the capital equipment to be purchased, the quantity of materials, and the size of the labour force.

4

(i) The committee would comprise those executives with responsibilities for the main functional activities of: Marketing and Sales; Purchasing; Production; Personnel; Accounting and Administration; Maintenance; Transport; Research and Development.

(ii) The main advantages of a budget committee are that all major sections of the organisation's activities are represented – the budget therefore reflects their collective responses to the tasks of planning and control; since all sections are represented, commitment to the budget is likely to be greater than if it were merely imposed; approaches to the budgeting process are likely to be standardised; problems which might arise are likely to be identified sooner, and solutions are likely to be those that are acceptable to those executives who have to carry them out.

(iii) You should explain four of the duties of the budget committee, explaining why each is necessary, and why a committee approach might be better than if the duties were carried out by one selected executive.

5

(a) You should identify and explain clearly the objectives of budgetary control. Two of these have especial bearing upon the problem; the features of measuring performance, and motivating managers.

(b) It is important to show how any advice you offer will overcome the company's management problem, *whilst at the same time* achieving the objectives of a budgetary control system. You might, therefore, wish to suggest the establishment of a budget committee, comprising all the senior managers, so that they are involved in the setting of the budgets for the ensuing period: if they are involved at an early stage, they are more likely to be supportive of the budget figures. Then you might suggest that during the period, regular – monthly (?) – meetings are held with the senior managers to discuss actual against planned performance, and to decide on courses of action. By involving senior managers in this way you may resurrect the degree of commitment which the chairman requires.

6 Functional budgets are often prepared by using the figures for the previous year as a basis, and then amending the figures to allow for inflation, or for planned changes in activity. *Zero base budgeting* does not do this: it begins each year by building the budget up from the very beginning. Each activity or function is closely examined, and alternative courses are studied. In this way, errors or inefficiencies which might have crept into the budgets for earlier years are not carried forward.

The technique is especially applicable where overhead expenditure makes up the larger share of the budget – as with Marketing and Sales, Administration, Research and Development.

With this technique, it is often useful to have managers study those areas of activity which impact upon their own areas, so that they can place the whole process into some form of perspective.

In building up the budget, the budget manager discusses each manager's budget individually with the manager concerned, questioning each item that is to be included.

8

			(£000)	(£000)
Sales: £1,680 + 25% + 2.5%				2152.5
Less:				
Direct materials: £500 + 25% + 8%			675	
Direct labour: £360 + 25% + 10%			495	
Production overhead: variable	£120 + 25%	150		
fixed	£220 + £15	235		
			385	
				1555.0
				597.5
Less:				
General administration:	£100 + £15		115	
Marketing: variable	£84 + 25%		105	
fixed	£166 + £35		201	
				421.0
				176.5

Profit.

Note: Assumes that variable marketing expenses vary in relation to the volume of sales.

A TUTOR'S ANSWER

Questions requiring the compilation of a cash budget are popular at all levels of examination: the higher the level, the more complicated are the calculations necessary. The following answer shows the basic steps to be followed in questions of this type.

7
(a)

	June £000	July £000	August £000
Receipts Schedule			
Debtors	54	45	63
Cash	7	6	5
	61	51	68
Payments Schedule			
Materials	30	25	35
Wages	12	10	9
Overhead	12	16	14
Commission	2.25	3.15	2.7
Loans	25		
Machines		15	15
	81.25	69.15	75.7
Cash Budget			
Balance	22	1.75	(16.4)
Add receipts	61	51.00	68.0
	83	52.75	51.6
Less payments	81.25	69.15	75.7
Balance	1.75	(16.40)	(24.1)

The Receipts schedule is used to total the monthly expected cash inflows. The Payments schedule identifies the planned cash outgoings. The monthly totals from the two schedules are combined in the cash budget to give an opening and closing cash balance as planned for each month. No matter how complicated is the question, this form of layout will ensure that you have included all the relevant figures, and will make checking of totals easy.

(b) Recognition over recent years of importance of liquidity, especially of cash flows. Official recognition in 1975 with SSAP 10 recommending publication of a Statement of Sources and Application of Funds. Examples of companies who have become insolvent because of inadequate cash flows: Rolls Royce, De Lorean, etc. Problem of overtrading – i.e. where a business enters into commitments which are greater than its short term assets.

Your answer should also explain the benefits of cash budgets, as detailed in the text above.

A STEP FURTHER

Arnold and Hope, *Accounting for Management Decisions*. Prentice Hall, Chs 14 and 15.

Daff, *Cost and Management Accounting*. Woodhead Faulkner, Ch. 7.

Drury, *Management and Cost Accounting*. Van Nostrand Reinhold, Ch. 15.

Harvey and Nettleton, *Management Accounting*. Mitchell Beazley, Ch. 5.

Lucey, *Costing*. D. P. Publications. Ch. 23.

Lucey, *Management Accounting*. D. P. Publications. Chs 7 and 10.

Norkett, *Management Accounting*. Pitman, Ch. 8.

Riddle, *Stage I Cost Accounting*. Northwick, Ch. 7.

Chapter 13

Standard costing

Standard costing is a topic that appears in virtually all examinations at whatever level. As with budgetary control, standard costing acts as a direct aid to management control, and as such, it is an important topic for accounting and management students alike.

Discussive questions include:

1. Definition of terms, and comparison of concepts.
2. Description of the recording systems necessary for the operation of a standard costing system.
3. Examination of the advantages of standard costing for management control.
4. Interpretation of the meaning of variances produced by calculation.

Computational questions cover the calculation of variances by either algebraic or graphical means.

STANDARD COSTING

Standard costing is an accounting technique which uses pre-set standards for costs and revenues, and which uses these standards for control purposes through the analysis of *variances*.

A *standard cost* is a predetermined calculation of planned cost levels under particular working conditions. The standards are compiled from various assessments of the cost elements, and this may involve:

- technical assessments, of what the plant and machinery can reasonably be expected to produce;
- assessments of the likely quantity of raw materials, and labour required to achieve the planned output;

- assessments of the costs of materials, labour, and overheads during the period under review, and for the output as planned.

Using these assessments, standards per unit of output are agreed for:

(a) direct material costs;
(b) direct labour costs;
(c) overhead costs.

When actual costs incurred are compared to the pre-set standards, *variances* arise. Thus, the method is sometimes called *variance accounting*.

Where the actual costs incurred are greater than those planned, an adverse or unfavourable variance results; when the actual costs are lower than those planned, a favourable variance arises.

SETTING STANDARDS

The key to a successful system of standard costing lies in the setting of the standards. If the maximum possible standards are used as bench marks, it is unlikely that these will be attained except in very unusual circumstances. The standards will thus be seen as barely attainable, and the whole system within the company may be brought into disrepute.

If standards are set upon the basis of current practice – or past experience – they may incorporate many inefficient working practices that have built up over years. The standards become too easy to reach, and the motivational elements of the system tend to suffer.

It is far better to base the standards upon what it is reasonable to expect efficient working to be. In doing this, it will be necessary to take advice from those very managers whose performance will be measured by the system; and experience indicates that people find such measures more acceptable if they themselves have had some part to play in the setting of the performance levels.

VARIANCE ANALYSIS

When the standard costing system has produced the variances, it is necessary to analyse the results. Variance analysis, therefore, constitutes the examination of all those influences which may have caused the variances to occur; and the identification of the management action necessary to rectify matters.

In this respect, the concept of *management by exception* applies. Management by exception assumes that for the majority of the time, the majority of the firm's activities are proceeding as planned. Managers can therefore concentrate their attention upon those few areas where problems are arising; since these are likely to be the exceptions, the management task is simplified.

Note that management by exception is a deliberate and planned approach to studying the differences between planned activity and actual activity. Management by crisis occurs where management's attention is directed to crises as they occur, with no planned approach towards dealing with problems.

MATERIAL VARIANCES

Material variances arise where the actual cost of raw materials is different from what was planned. Such differences may arise because more (or less) was paid for the materials than was planned – a *price variance* – or because more (or less) of the materials were used than was allowed for – a *usage variance*. Where materials are used in combination, the usage variance can be further divided into a *material mix variance* and a *material yield variance*.

The necessary formulae are:

Total material variance	=	(Standard usage × Standard price) − (Actual usage × Actual price)
Price variance	=	(Standard price − Actual price) × Actual quantity
Usage variance	=	(Standard quantity − Actual quantity) × Standard price
Material mix variance	=	(Standard mix − Actual mix) × Standard price
Material yield variance	=	(Standard yield − Actual yield) × Standard cost

The relationship between the variances is:

Total material variance = Price variance + Usage variance

Usage variance = Mix variance + Yield variance

LABOUR VARIANCES

Labour variances arise where the actual cost of direct labour is different from what was planned. Such differences may arise because a greater (or less) wage rate was paid than was planned – a *wage rate variance* – or because the labour hours taken were greater (or less) than was planned – an *efficiency variance*.

The formulae to be used are:

Total labour variance	=	(Standard hours × Standard rate) − (Actual hours × Actual rate)
Wage rate variance	=	(Standard wage rate − Actual wage rate) × Actual hours
Efficiency variance	=	(Standard hours − Actual hours) × Standard wage rate

The relationship between the variances is:

Total labour variance = Wage rate variance + Efficiency variance

OVERHEAD VARIANCES

Overhead variances arise where the actual overhead incurred is greater (or less) than that planned. Overhead variances comprise *fixed overhead variances* and *variable overhead variances*, each of which can be further subdivided. The variable overhead variance can be divided into the *variable overhead efficiency variance*, and the *variable overhead expenditure variance*. The fixed overhead variance can be divided into the *fixed overhead efficiency variance*, and the *fixed overhead volume variance*.

The formulae to use are:

Variable overhead Efficiency variance	=	$\Big($ Standard hours for production achieved	−	Actual hours taken $\Big)$	× Standard variable overhead rate
Variable overhead Expenditure variance	=	$\Big($ Actual variable overhead	−	Actual hours $\Big)$	× Variable overhead rate
Fixed overhead expenditure variance	=	Budgeted fixed overhead	−	Actual fixed overhead	
Fixed overhead volume variance	=	$\Big($ Actual quantity of work done	−	Standard quantity of work done $\Big)$	× Standard fixed overhead rate

The quantity of work done is measured in terms of *standard hours*. A standard hour is not a measure of time: it is a measure of the quantity of work achievable at the standard performance level. It is usually expressed in terms of a standard unit of work in a standard period of time.

The relationship between the variances is:

Total overhead variance	=	$\Big($ Standard fixed overhead + Standard variable overhead $\Big)$	−	$\Big($ Actual fixed overhead + Actual variable overhead $\Big)$
Total fixed overhead variance	=	Fixed overhead expenditure variance	+	Volume variance
Total variable overhead variance	=	Variable overhead expenditure variance	+	Variable overhead efficiency variance

Overhead expenditure variances arise where bought-in supplies and services are greater (or less) than was planned, where the cost of indirect labour was different from planned, or where services have been in some way misused.

The efficiency variance is an extension of the labour efficiency variance, and may arise because of the use of a different grade of labour than was intended, because supervision was better than (or worse than) was planned, or because of material or equipment problems (or advantages).

The volume variance arises because of variations in production, resulting in more (or less) overhead being absorbed than was planned.

GRAPHICAL PRESENTATION

Fig. 13.1 shows how it is possible to depict the differences between actual and standard costs by means of a series of graphs.

In (a) OABC is the standard cost, and ODEF is the actual cost. Wherever the rectangle for actual cost lies outside of the rectangle for standard cost, an unfavourable – or adverse – variance is indicated. Where the rectangle for actual cost lies within the rectangle for standard cost, a favourable variance is shown.

In (a) the area ADEG depicts an adverse price variance; and FGBC depicts a favourable usage variance.

Graph (b) applies to labour variances, OTUV is the standard cost; OWXY is the actual cost; WTUZ shows a favourable wage rate variance; VZXY shows an adverse efficiency variance.

Fig. 13.1   Variance graphs

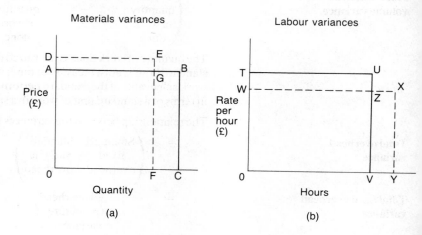

(a)

(b)

USEFUL APPLIED MATERIALS

The following is an example of a profit and loss statement presented under standard costing. The product should have generated sales of £41,000, earning a profit of £11,200 (£41,000 − £30,000). In fact, because of the variances incurred during the period, actual profit earned was £9,710.

162

Profit and Loss Statement
for January 19–8

	(£)	(£)	(£)
Budgeted sales		41,000	
Less standard cost of sales	30,000		
stock adjustment	200		
		29,800	
			11,200

Variances

	(£)	
Sales: Price	810 (A)	
: Volume	150 (F)	
		660 (A)
Direct materials: Price	100 (A)	
Mix	130 (A)	
Yield	110 (F)	
		120 (A)
Direct wages: Rate	340 (A)	
Mix	300 (F)	
Efficiency	600 (A)	
Yield	140 (F)	
		500 (A)
Variable overhead: Expenditure		100 (A)
Fixed overhead: Expenditure	180 (F)	
Productivity	390 (A)	
Yield	100 (F)	
		110 (A)
Total		1,490 (A)
Actual net profit		9,710

RECENT EXAMINATION QUESTIONS

Questions **1** and **2** test an understanding of the principles and terms of standard costing. Questions **3**, **5**, and **7** are calculation questions. Question **4** uses the graphical approach to determine variances, and question **6** examines the effects upon a Profit and Loss account. Question **7** has been selected for the *Tutor's Answer*.

1

(a) Define in the context of cost accounting the following terms:
  (i)   standard;
  (ii) standard cost;
  (iii) standard costing.

(5 marks)

(b) State:
  (i) the advantages; and
  (ii) the disadvantages

    that may be expected by using a system of standard costing.
                                                          (10 marks)

(c) Why may it be said that the analysis of overhead variances is more complex than the analysis of prime cost variances?

                                                           (3 marks)
                                          (RSA Stage III, June 1986)

2

(a) Describe briefly the information needed to compile the standard cost of a given product.

                                                           (6 marks)

(b) How is the information you have stated in your answer to (a) above used in the control of operating costs?

                                                           (8 marks)

(c) State the areas in which the standard cost of a product is used:

  (i) to assist management when it is making certain decisions;
  (ii) in the accounting work of the business.

                                                           (6 marks)
                                          (RSA Stage III, June 1985)

3 The technique of *variance accounting* is incorporated into the costing system used by BCD Limited. The following data relate to the month of May:

	Process 1	Process 2
Direct labour hours worked	2,500	8,000
Direct wages earned	£9,300	£33,300
Units produced	800	2,100
Standard hours per unit	3	4
Standard hourly rate	£3.80	£4.00

Calculate, for each process:

(i)   The standard direct labour cost per unit.

                                                           (2 marks)

(ii) The direct wages variance.

                                                           (4 marks)

(iii) The direct wage rate variance.

                                                           (4 marks)

(iv) The direct wages efficiency variance.

                                                           (4 marks)

(v)   The efficiency ratio.

                                                           (6 marks)
                                     (LCC Higher, Summer 1986)

4 This diagram reflects costs within a standard costing system. Assume that all the variances are unfavourable.

Fig. 13.2

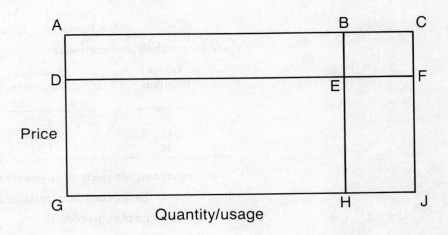

(a) State which rectangle(s) represent the:
   (i)   standard cost;
   (ii) actual cost;
   (iii) material price variance;
   (iv) material usage variance;
   (v)   material cost variance.

(9 marks)

Note: Your answer should be stated in the form of the letters representing each corner of each rectangle; it is not necessary to draw the diagram.

(CIMA Foundation, November 1984)

5 The standard direct material costs of each of the two products, J and K, made by E. Limited are based on the following data:

Direct material	Standard price per kilogram (£)	Standard quantity in kilograms per unit	
		Product J	Product K
F	3.00	5	4
G	2.50	6	8
H	4.00	2	3

During the month ended 31 March 1985, production was as follows:

Product J   300 units
Product K   250 units

and the materials consumed were:

Direct materials	Quantity in kilograms	Actual price per kilogram (£)
F	2,520	2.95
G	3,786	2.50
H	1,340	4.10

Using the information given above you are required to:

(a)   Calculate the standard direct material cost of:

  (i)   one unit of each product;

(4 marks)

  (ii)   the total products made.

(2 marks)

(b)   Ascertain the direct material cost variance in total, and for each material.

(6 marks)

(c)   Analyse the direct material cost variances obtained in answer to (b) above into:
  (i)   direct material price variances;

(4 marks)

  (ii)   direct material usage variances.

(4 marks)

(d)   State, with reasons, whether it is true that the variances you have calculated in answers to (c) (ii) above in respect of material H indicate that material losses in production were greater than those allowed for in the standard.

(2 marks)
(RSA Stage II, April 1985)

6   EB Jones Ltd operates a standard costing system. The budget for the year ended 20 June 1985 was to produce and sell 10,000 units of output. The standard cost sheet showed the following cost structure per unit:

Direct materials:	material A	10 kg at £1.00 kg
	material B	5 kg at £5.00 kg
Direct wages:	5 hours at £3.00 per hour	

Fixed production overhead absorption rate: 2 times direct wages.
Budgeted profit: 20 per cent of selling price.

Actual results were:

Materials consumed: material A 96,000 kg at £1.20 kg; material B 48,000
kg at £4.70 kg.
Direct wages : 46,000 hours at a wage rate of £3.20 per hour.
Fixed production overhead incurred: £290,000.

You are required to prepare the profit and loss statement for the year.
(ACEA Pt II, June 1985)

7 The information shown below is an extract from the previous period's
budget and standard cost data for the Machining Department in a
company manufacturing two products and which operates a full
absorption standard costing system.

	Product X	Product Y
Budgeted production	6,500 units	4,200 units
Standard machine hours allowed to process each product in the Machining Department	4 hours	7 hours

The department's overhead is applied to production by means of a
standard machine hour absorption rate and this is calculated at the
beginning of each period. The variable element of the previous period's
absorption rate was £1.50 per standard machine hour, and the
department's total overheads for that period were budgeted to be
£207,750. The budget assumes that one standard machine hour should be
produced in one actual hour of machining time.
    The actual results in the Machining Department for the previous
period were:

Actual machining time	54,000
Production: Product X	7,200 units
Product Y	4,000 units
Actual overheads incurred:	
Fixed	£120,550
Variable	£87,600

(a) Calculate the following variances from the standard/budget cost
    which occurred in the Machining Department during the previous
    period:

    Fixed overhead volume variance.
    Fixed overhead expenditure variance.
    Variable overhead expenditure variance.

(10 marks)

(b) Discuss in detail the possible reasons for the fixed overhead volume variance.

(7 marks)

(c) Calculate the Machining Department's total flexed overhead budget for the actual level of production in the previous period and explain the difference between this total budgeted amount and the total production overhead absorbed by the department in the period.

(5 marks)

(ACCA Level 1, December 1984)

For a description of flexible budgets, see Chapter 12 above.

OUTLINE ANSWERS

1

(a) (i)   A standard is a predetermined measurable quantity set in defined conditions, against which actual performance can be compared. They involve the application of human judgement, and are thus open to debate.

(ii) A standard cost is a predetermined calculation of how much costs should be under certain conditions.

(iii) Standard costing is a technique which uses standards for costs and revenues for the purpose of control through variance analysis.

(b) The advantages of standard costing are that it enables comparisons to be made between planned activity and actual performance; and it enables responsibilities for performance to be identified.

The disadvantages of standard costing revolve around the issue of comparing actual performance with the standard. If the actual conditions under which actual performance takes place are different from those which were assumed, then a comparison of actual with planned performance is not comparing like with like.

(c) Overhead variances arise through differences between the actual amount of overhead incurred, and the amount which is charged to production through *previously determined overhead absorption rates*. Whereas prime cost variances arise because of differences between actual price and/or quantity of the prime cost element.

2

(a) Information is needed on the costs likely to be incurred for labour, materials, and overheads – within a particular environment. This information comprises the quantities and the likely prices of the elements of prime cost; and an agreed set of assumptions – and costings – concerning overheads.

(b) The information is used to control operating costs by way of variance analysis. This involves examining the factors which have caused the differences, with a view to eliminating inefficiencies.

(c) Standard costing helps in management decision-making by revealing any shortcomings either in actual performance, or in the planned performance as agreed.

In the accounting work of the business, standard costing provides yardsticks for costs against which actual costs can be compared.

3

		Process 1	Process 2
(i)	Standard direct labour cost per unit (£):	11.40	16.00
(ii)	Direct wages variance (£):	180 (A)	300 (F)
(iii)	Direct wage rate variance (£):	200 (F)	1,300 (A)
(iv)	Direct wages efficiency variance (£):	380 (A)	1,600 (F)
(v)	Efficiency ratio	96	105

The standard direct labour cost per unit is calculated by multiplying the standard hours per unit by the standard hourly rate. Thus, $3 \times £3.80 = £11.40$; and $4 \times £4.00 = £16.00$.

The direct wages variance is the standard cost less the actual cost. The standard cost is the number of units produced multiplied by the standard direct labour cost per unit – which was calculated in (i). Thus, in Process 1, $([£11.40 \times 800] - £9,300) = -£180$; in Process 2, $([£16.00 \times 2,100] - £33,300) = £300$.

The direct wage rate variance requires the use of the relevant formulae. In Process 1, $(£3.80 - [£9,300 \div 2,500]) \times 2,500 = £200$. In Process 2, $(£4.00 - [£33,300 \div 8,000]) \times 8,000 = -£1,300$.

The direct wages efficiency variance is: Process 1, $([800 \times 3] - 2,500) \times £3.80 = -£380$; Process 2, $([2,100 \times 4] - 8,000) \times £4.00 = £1,600$.

The direct wage rate variance plus the direct wages efficiency variance should equal the direct wages variance. For Process 1, $£200 - £380 = -£180$; for Process 2, $-£1,300 + £1,600 = £300$.

The efficiency ratio is calculated by the formula:

$$\frac{\text{Standard hours of production achieved} \times 100}{\text{Actual number of direct working hours}}$$

Thus, Process 1 =

$$\frac{(800 \times 3) \times 100}{2,500} = 96$$

Process 2 =

$$\frac{(2,100 \times 4) \times 100}{8,000} = 105$$

4

(i)   Standard cost: DEHG
(ii) Actual cost: ACJG
(iii) Material price variance: ACFD
(iv) Material usage variance: EFJH
(v)   Material cost variance: ACFD + EFJH

5(a)

Material		Product J				Product K		
	Price (£)	Quantity kg	Output units	Total (£)	Price (£)	Quantity kg	Output units	Total (£)
F	3.00	5	300	4,500	3.00	4	250	3,000
G	2.50	6	300	4,500	2.50	8	250	5,000
H	4.00	2	300	2,400	4.00	3	250	3,000
				11,400				11,000

Standard direct material cost per unit: J = £11,400 ÷ 300 = £38

K = £11,000 ÷ 250 = £44

(b)

Material	Standard cost			Actual cost			Variance
	Product J (£)	+ K (£)	Total (£)	Price (£)	Quantity kg	Total (£)	(£)
F	4,500	3,000	7,500	2.95	2,520	7,434	66
G	4,500	5,000	9,500	2.50	3,786	9,465	35
H	2,400	3,000	5,400	4.10	1,340	5,494	−94

Total direct material cost variance: 7

(c) *Direct material price variances*:

Material				Price variances		
	Std Price (£)	−	Act Price (£)	×	Act Quant kg	Variance (£)
F	3.00		2.95		2,520	126
G	2.50		2.50		3,786	–
H	4.00		4.10		1,340	−134
Total						−8

Direct material usage variances:

Material				Usage variances		
	Std Quant kg	−	Act Quant kg	×	Std Price (£)	Variance (£)
F	2,500		2,520		3.00	−60
G	3,800		3,786		2.50	35
H	1,350		1,340		4.00	40
Total						15

The figures can be checked by ensuring that the sum of the price variances plus the sum of the usage variances equals the total direct material cost variance: $(-8) + 15 = 7$.

Note that the standard quantities have been calculated by multiplying the actual outputs by the standard kilograms per unit. Hence,

Material	Quantity Used in Product		Total
	J	K	kg
F	(300 × 5)	+ (250 × 4)	2,500
G	(300 × 6)	+ (250 × 8)	3,800
H	(300 × 2)	+ (250 × 3)	1,350

(d) Material H shows a positive or favourable usage variance of £40. This could indicate that the work force was more skilled in using the material than usual; it could indicate a better quality of material; a better use of machines; or better supervision. The variances of themselves will not indicate the reasons for the differences; they merely identify the areas where perhaps questions should be asked.

6

EB Jones Ltd
Profit and Loss Statement for the year ended 20 June 1985
(£000)

Budgeted sales		1,000.0	
Less standard cost of sales		800	
Budgeted profit			200.0
Variances:			
Direct materials (A)	15.2 (A)		
(B)	24.4 (F)		
		9.2 (F)	
Labour		2.8 (F)	
Fixed o/h		10.0 (F)	
			22.0 (F)
Actual profit			222.0

7   Previous period's budgeted total machine hours:
Product X (6,500 units × 4 hours) = 26,000
Product Y (4,200 units × 7 hours) = 29,400

55,400

Budgeted variable overheads:
55,400 standard machine hours × £1.50 per hour   =   £83,100

Budgeted fixed overheads:
Budgeted total overheads   −   budgeted variable overheads
£207,750   −   £83,100   = £124,650

Budgeted fixed overhead absorption rate:
Budgeted fixed overheads   ÷   budgeted standard machine hours
£124,650   ÷   55,400   =   £2.25
per machine hour

(a)   Calculation of fixed overhead variances:

Standard cost of actual production:
Product X, (7,200 units × 4 hours)   =   28,800
Product Y (4,000 units × 7 hours)   =   28,000

56,800 m/hrs

56,800 std mach hrs × £2.25	=	£127,800 . . . . .(i)
Budgeted fixed overheads	=	£124,650 . . . . .(ii)
Fixed overhead volume variance (i)–(ii)	=	£3,150 (F)
Actual overhead expenditure	=	£120,550 . . . . (iii)
Fixed overhead expenditure variance (ii)–(iii)	=	£4,100 (F)
Calculation of variable overhead variances:		
56,800 std mach hrs × £1.50	=	£85,200 . . . . .(iv)
Actual overhead expenditure	=	£87,600 . . . . .(v)
Variable overhead expenditure variance (iv–(v)	=	£2,400 (A)

(b)   The favourable fixed overhead volume variance has arisen because
the actual production (at 56,800 standard machine hours) was
greater than that which was planned 55,400 standard machine hours.
      The increased output was probably a result of increased
demand. Such an increase in demand would normally have resulted
in an increase in machine hours, except that some of the increase was
absorbed by improved efficiency; 56,800 standard hours were
produced by working 54,000 machine hours.
      The actual number of machine hours worked, was also less than
the number budgeted for: 54,000 actually worked, whereas 55,400
were planned. The reasons for this could have been either improved
efficiency and/or a reduction in the capacity available (in terms of
machine hours). Improved efficiency may have come about because
of employees working harder, better production planning, improved
supervision, a change of work practices.

(c) The previous period's flexed budget for the Machining Department:

	(£)
Budgeted fixed overheads	124,650
Flexed variable overheads:	
56,800 std hrs × £1.50	85,200
Total flexed budget	209,850

The difference between the flexed overhead budget and the total production overhead absorbed is caused by the treatment of fixed overheads. The flexed budget will show fixed overheads at a constant amount over a reasonable range of activity, whilst the fixed overhead element of production overhead absorbed will vary directly with the level of production activity.

A STEP FURTHER

Arnold and Hope, *Accounting for Management Decisions*. Prentice Hall, Ch. 16.
Daff, *Cost and Management Accounting*. Woodhead Faulkner, Ch. 8.
Drury, *Management and Cost Accounting*. Van Nostrand Reinhold, Chs 17 and 18.
Lucey, *Costing*. D. P. Publications, Chs 24–26.
Lucey, *Management Accounting*. D. P. Publications, Chs 11 and 12.
Norkett, *Management Accounting*. Pitman, Ch. 9.
Riddle, *Stage I Cost Accounting*. Northwick, Ch. 8.

Investment appraisal

GETTING STARTED

Not all syllabuses include this topic, especially syllabuses at the more elementary levels: do check whether your examination requires a knowledge of investment appraisal.

Discussive questions tend to comprise:

1. A definition of terms, and a comparison of concepts.
2. A discussion of the merits and demerits of discounting and non-discounting methods of investment appraisal.
3. The selection of desirable projects given particular criteria, and justification for the choice made.

Computational questions include:

1. The calculation of a company's cost of capital.
2. The calculation of Net Present Values, Internal Rates of Return (yield), and Payback periods.

The calculations are usually made with the help of tables: a knowledge of the underlying formulae is rarely required.

ESSENTIAL PRINCIPLES

Investment is any application of money – or money's worth – which is intended to provide a return by way of interest, dividend or capital appreciation. *Capital investment* is investment in specific fixed assets. *Investment appraisal* is the process of evaluating (i) any proposed investment whether in fixed assets, or in other resources, and (ii) the benefits to be gained from the investment. Note that investment may or may not require the acquisition of fixed assets: it may merely be a decision to commit resources to some course of action, as with Research and Development.

The methods for evaluating capital investment projects fall into two general groups, depending upon whether or not they take account of the *time value* of money:

- non-discounting techniques – such as payback – which ignore time values;
- discounting techniques – such as net present value, and yield – which do consider time values.

COMPOUND INTEREST

The time value of money has to do with the existence of *interest*. With *compound interest*, the interest earned by an investment is calculated upon the principal sum invested, *plus* the accrued interest. With *simple interest*, the interest accruing is calculated solely upon the principal sum.

Interest has the effect of making a sum of money payable in the future worth less than that same sum of money payable immediately, since money received now can be invested at interest. By the time any future date comes around, the investment will have grown by the amount of the interest.

The notion of investment appraisal is based upon the idea of compound interest. The calculation of compound interest can be carried out by means of the necessary formula, but examination bodies nowadays tend to concentrate upon the use of relevant tables. Provided that you understand the workings of compound interest, it is usually not necessary to memorise the required formula.

PRESENT VALUE

Compound tables are used to determine the growth of an investment between a period now, and another at some time in the future. Compound tables, therefore, contain factors greater than one, and these factors increase through the table, reflecting the growth of the initial investment as time accrues (Table 14.1).

Table 14.1 Compound amount of 1

Period	1%	2%	3%	4%	5%	6%	7%	8%	9%	10%	11%	12%	13%	14%	15%
1	1.010	1.020	1.030	1.040	1.050	1.060	1.070	1.080	1.090	1.100	1.110	1.120	1.130	1.140	1.150
2	1.020	1.040	1.061	1.082	1.102	1.124	1.145	1.166	1.188	1.210	1.232	1.254	1.277	1.300	1.322
3	1.030	1.061	1.093	1.125	1.158	1.191	1.225	1.260	1.295	1.331	1.368	1.405	1.443	1.482	1.521
4	1.041	1.082	1.126	1.170	1.216	1.262	1.311	1.360	1.412	1.464	1.518	1.575	1.631	1.689	1.749
5	1.051	1.104	1.159	1.217	1.276	1.338	1.403	1.469	1.539	1.611	1.685	1.762	1.843	1.925	2.011
6	1.062	1.126	1.194	1.265	1.340	1.419	1.501	1.587	1.677	1.772	1.870	1.974	2.083	2.195	2.313
7	1.072	1.149	1.230	1.316	1.407	1.504	1.606	1.714	1.828	1.949	2.076	2.211	2.353	2.502	2.660
8	1.083	1.172	1.267	1.369	1.477	1.594	1.718	1.851	1.993	2.144	2.304	2.476	2.659	2.853	3.059
9	1.094	1.195	1.305	1.423	1.551	1.689	1.838	1.999	2.172	2.358	2.557	2.773	3.005	3.252	3.803
10	1.105	1.219	1.344	1.480	1.629	1.791	1.967	2.159	2.367	2.594	2.838	3.106	3.396	3.707	4.046
11	1.116	1.243	1.384	1.539	1.710	1.898	2.105	2.332	2.580	2.853	3.150	3.479	3.838	4.226	4.652
12	1.127	1.268	1.426	1.601	1.796	2.012	2.252	2.518	2.813	3.138	3.497	3.896	4.337	4.818	5.350
13	1.138	1.294	1.469	1.665	1.886	2.133	2.410	2.720	3.066	3.452	3.882	4.363	4.901	5.492	6.153
14	1.149	1.319	1.513	1.732	1.980	2.261	2.579	2.937	3.342	3.797	4.309	4.887	5.538	6.261	7.076
15	1.161	1.346	1.558	1.801	2.079	2.397	2.759	3.172	3.642	4.177	4.783	5.474	6.258	7.138	8.137

Present value tables are used to determine what must be invested now in order to grow to a specified amount by the end of a particular period in the future. Present value tables contain factors less than one, and these factors decrease through the table, reflecting the diminution in current investment necessary to secure a particular sum as the pay-off recedes into the future (Table 14.2).

Table 14.2 Present value of 1

Period	1%	2%	3%	4%	5%	6%	7%	8%	9%	10%
1	0.990	0.980	0.971	0.961	0.952	0.943	0.935	0.926	0.917	0.909
2	0.980	0.961	0.943	0.925	0.907	0.890	0.873	0.857	0.842	0.826
3	0.971	0.942	0.915	0.889	0.864	0.840	0.816	0.794	0.772	0.751
4	0.961	0.924	0.889	0.855	0.823	0.792	0.763	0.735	0.708	0.683
5	0.951	0.906	0.863	0.822	0.784	0.747	0.713	0.681	0.650	0.621
6	0.942	0.888	0.838	0.790	0.746	0.705	0.666	0.630	0.596	0.564
7	0.933	0.871	0.813	0.760	0.711	0.665	0.623	0.583	0.547	0.513
8	0.923	0.853	0.789	0.731	0.677	0.627	0.582	0.540	0.502	0,467
9	0.914	0.837	0.766	0.703	0.645	0.592	0.544	0.500	0.460	0.424
10	0.905	0.820	0.744	0.676	0.614	0.588	0.508	0.463	0.422	0.386
11	0.896	0.804	0.722	0.650	0.585	0.527	0.475	0.429	0.388	0.350
12	0.887	0.788	0.701	0.625	0.557	0.497	0.444	0.397	0.356	0.319
13	0.879	0.773	0.681	0.601	0.530	0.469	0.415	0.368	0.326	0.290
14	0.870	0.758	0.661	0.577	0.505	0.442	0.388	0.340	0.299	0.263
15	0.861	0.743	0.642	0.555	0.481	0.417	0.362	0.315	0.275	0.239

Period	11%	12%	13%	14%	15%	16%	17%	18%	19%	20%
1	0.901	0.893	0.885	0.877	0.870	0.862	0.855	0.847	0.840	0.833
2	0.812	0.797	0.783	0.769	0.756	0.743	0.731	0.718	0.706	0.694
3	0.731	0.712	0.693	0.675	0.658	0.641	0.624	0.609	0.593	0.571
4	0.659	0.636	0.613	0.592	0.572	0.552	0.534	0.516	0.499	0.482
5	0.594	0.567	0.543	0.519	0.497	0.476	0.456	0.437	0.419	0.402
6	0.535	0.507	0.480	0.456	0.432	0.410	0.390	0.370	0.352	0.335
7	0.482	0.452	0.425	0.400	0.376	0.354	0.333	0.314	0.296	0.279
8	0.434	0.404	0.376	0.351	0.327	0.305	0.285	0.266	0.249	0.233
9	0.391	0.361	0.333	0.308	0.284	0.263	0.243	0.226	0.209	0.194
10	0.352	0.322	0.295	0.270	0.247	0.227	0.208	0.191	0.176	0.162
11	0.317	0.287	0.261	0.237	0.215	0.195	0.178	0.162	0.148	0.135
12	0.289	0.257	0.231	0.208	0.187	0.169	0.152	0.137	0.124	0.112
13	0.258	0.229	0.204	0.182	0.163	0.145	0.130	0.116	0.104	0.094
14	0.232	0.205	0.181	0.160	0.141	0.125	0.111	0.099	0.088	0.078
15	0.209	0.183	0.160	0.140	0.123	0.108	0.095	0.084	0.074	0.065

VALUATION OF FIXED ASSETS

The value of fixed assets largely depends upon the purposes for which the valuation is required. One way of valuing a fixed asset is in terms of its earning power; in terms of the increased net cash in-flows which it will generate. After all, cash is invested in capital assets now in the hope of receiving cash in-flows in the future.

From the discussion on compound interest and present values, we know that monies received in the future are worth less now than monies received now; and that the further into the future we go, the less this present value becomes. By adjusting the estimated future net cash in-flows for this diminution in value, we can derive the total value of a particular investment project in terms of the present value of its expected cash flows.

This method of valuation is achieved simply by calculating the present value of each period's net in-flows, and by then adding these present values together. For ease of calculation, the method implicitly assumes that the in-flows accrue at the end of each period. The activity of adjusting future in-flows to allow for the time value of money is known as *discounting*.

Note that an investment project can be anything from the purchase of one small machine, to the construction of a whole new factory.

NET PRESENT VALUE

A project's *Net Present Value* (NPV) is calculated by subtracting the initial outlay from the total present value of the in-flows. In terms of investment appraisal, any project which gives a positive NPV is acceptable; and any project which gives a negative NPV is not. Where the number of acceptable projects exceeds the number which the firm can undertake, those with higher positive NPVs are preferred to those with lower positive NPVs.

INTERNAL RATE OF RETURN (YIELD)

A project's *Internal Rate of Return* (IRR) is that discount rate at which the project's NPV just equals zero. Projects which must be financed by borrowed money should only be considered where their IRR is greater than the interest which must be paid on the loans.

COST OF CAPITAL

The general discount rate to be used in investment appraisal should normally be the company's weighted average cost of capital. This method recognises that different forms of finance have different costs, and in calculating an overall rate for the firm, it acknowledges their relative importance to the company.

Where debenture interest is an allowable expense against corporation tax – and whether it is or not depends upon the taxation regulations ruling at any particular time – an adjustment is necessary to allow for the tax reduction. The formula to be used is:

$$R = r(1-t)$$

Where R is the after tax cost of the debentures, r is the pre-tax return on the debentures expressed as a percentage, and t is the tax rate expressed as a decimal.

Where debenture interest is an allowable expense against corporation tax, there are advantages in incorporating loan capital within a company's capital structure, since part of the cost of servicing the debt is met from taxation. However, the perception of the investing public places limits upon just how far a company can increase its debt capital. The more debt it has, the greater the risk that the company's profits will be unable to meet the interest payments; the investment becomes risky for debenture holders, and for holders of the ordinary shares, and each class of investor will begin to demand increases in returns in order to compensate for the increased risk.

177

After a certain point, the disadvantages of these increased returns begin to outweigh the advantages of increased loan capital.

Where debenture interest is not an allowable expense against taxation, there may still be an advantage in including some loan capital within a company's capital structure, since debenture holders usually demand a smaller return than do the holders of ordinary shares -- because debentures are less risky than are ordinary shares. The existence of such less expensive capital therefore reduces the company's overall cost of capital.

A company which has a high proportion of loan capital is known as *highly geared*; one which has a low proportion of loan capital is known as *low geared*. A company's *debt capacity* is the extent to which it can raise loan finance.

PAYBACK METHOD

The *payback* method of investment appraisal makes no allowance for time values: the project's income stream is simply added to determine how long the project will take to pay for itself. Payback may be used on its own, or it may be used with other methods, especially where there is particular uncertainty over future cash inflows.

USEFUL APPLIED MATERIAL

Evidence on industrys' use of the different methods of investment appraisal was sought by Richard Pike in 1980–81. The following table taken from his results, shows the methods used, and whether firms used one, two, three or four approaches in combination. Evidence for 1975 is shown for comparison.

Note that the *Average Accounting Rate of Return* method divides the average net income by the average investment, expressed as a percentage. The method ignores time values. This method does not generally appear in examination syllabuses at elementary and intermediate levels.

Table 14.3

Investment Appraisal:
Evaluation Methods Used

	Companies			
	1980–81		*1975*	
No method	0		5	4%
Single method				
a	17		16	
b	12		19	
c	6		8	
d	4		1	
	39	26%	44	33%
Two methods				
ab	17		14	
ac	18		14	
ad	9		7	
bc	4		1	
bd	2		3	
cd	5		4	
	55	37%	43	32%
Three methods				
abc	16		10	
abd	9		8	
acd	15		11	
bcd	1		1	
	41	27%	30	22%
Four methods				
abcd	15	10%	12	9%
Total	150	100	134	100

Key a: payback
b: average accounting rate of return
c: internal rate of return
d: net present value.

(From Pike: *Capital Budgeting in the 1980s*)

Question **1** tests an understanding of the principles of investment appraisal, and a knowledge of terms. Question **2** asks for a comparison of discounting and non-discounting methods. Question **3** seeks an explanation of the relationship of NPV and IRR; and question **4** – which has been chosen for the *Tutor's Answer* – requires the calculation of a company's after-tax cost of capital, and the application of this to investment appraisal.

1   You have been appointed as chief management accountant of a well-established company with a brief to improve the quality of information supplied for management decision-making. As a first task you have decided to examine the system used for providing information for capital investment decisions. You find that discounted cash flow techniques are used in a mechanical fashion with no apparent understanding of the figures produced. The most recent example of an investment appraisal produced by the accounting department showed a positive Net Present Value of £35,000 for a five-year life project when discounted at 14 per cent which you are informed 'was the rate charged on the bank loan raised to finance the investment'. You note that the appraisal did not include any consideration of the effects of inflation nor was their any form of risk analysis.

(a)   Explain the meaning of Net Present Value.

(4 marks)

(b)   Comment on the appropriateness or otherwise of the rate used.

(4 marks)

(c)   State whether you agree with the treatment of inflation and, if not, explain how you would deal with inflation in investment appraisals.

(6 marks)

(d)   Explain what is meant by 'risk analysis' and describe ways this could be carried out in investment appraisals and what benefits (if any) this would bring.

(6 marks)

(CIMA Stage 3 Specimen, 1986)

2   Compare and contrast discounting and non-discounting methods of investment appraisal. Illustrate your answer with examples.

(20 marks)

(ULSEB, 'A' Level, January 1986)

3

(a)   Explain the relationship between Net Present Value (NPV) and Yield (Internal Rate of Return).

(4 marks)

(b)   A firm is considering an investment project costing £12,500. The estimated annual cash flows accruing at the end of each year are:

Year 1	£2,500	Year 3	£5,700
Year 2	£4,600	Year 4	£7,000

If the company has to borrow money to finance the project, is the maximum rate of interest it should pay for finance 16 per cent; 18 per cent; 20 per cent? Give reasons for your answer.

(11 marks)

(ULSEB, 'A' Level, June 1986)

4 A company has the following capital structure with each type of finance having the cost shown:

(£000)

Ordinary shares	(20%)	1,000
Preference shares	(16%)	600
Debentures	(10%)	400

Debenture interest is allowable against corporation tax; the latter for the company is 40 per cent.

The company currently has three investment projects under review, details of which are given below. However, only two of the projects can be undertaken in the immediate future.

Project	Arrow	Dart	Spear
Initial cost (£)	18,000	22,000	24,000
Cash flows (£)			
Year 1	7,000	6,500	8,200
Year 2	11,000	7,000	10,400
Year 3	11,300	8,500	10,800
Year 4	11,500	12,800	11,600
Year 5	11,900	14,300	12,000

(a) Calculate the company's cost of capital.

(5 marks)

(b) Rank the projects in order of preference using:

  (i) payback
  (ii) NPV (Net Present Value); use your answer to (a) as the discount rate.

(17 marks)

(c) State, with reasons, the two projects which you advise the company to select.

(8 marks)

(ULSEB, 'A' Level, June 1984)

OUTLINE ANSWERS

1

(a) Net Present Value (NPV) of a project is the amount by which the discounted values of the cash inflows exceed the present values of the cash outflows. Discounting is the term applied to amending cash flows to take account of the time value of money.

(b) The discount rate normally used to amend cash flows is the company's weighted average cost of capital: the use of the rate charged on a bank loan may serve as a rough approximation, but it is not recommended for general use, since the company's weighted average cost of capital may be substantially different.

(c) Allowing for inflation – as well as for the time value of money – is difficult, since forecasts on inflation are not easy to make. Two approaches may be used: (i) amend the residual cash flows by the estimated inflation rate; or (ii) amend each input and output by estimated inflation rates, so as to completely recalculate the net cash flows per period.

(d) No investment decisions are void of risk. Three approaches may be used to deal with risk: (i) increase the discount factor used in the calculations, so that the project only becomes acceptable when it produces higher income flows; (ii) reduce the income flows, thereby building in some safety margin; (iii) adopt some form of probabilistic analysis, by allocating probabilities to the best, worst, and most likely level of cash flows.

2 Discounting methods use time value of money; money accruing in the future has less value than money accruing now; effects of interest rates, irrespective of inflation; reduce a project's estimated net cash flows to allow for this.

With NPV deduct the initial cost from the total of the discounted cash flows; accept projects with positive NPVs, and reject those with negative NPVs; where projects give positive NPVs accept those with higher NPVs if choice is limited. Internal Rate of Return on project is that discount rate at which the NPV is zero; accept projects with an IRR greater than the cost of finance.

Payback does not use time values; it calculates the time the investment takes to pay for itself out of the revenues earned; the shorter the payback time, the more attractive is the project; it ignores income flows arising after the payback period.

3

(a) A project's NPV is zero when its net cash flows are discounted at its IRR.

(b) Interest rate

Year	Cash flows	(16%) Factor	Discounted	(18%) Factor	Discounted	(20%) Factor	Discounted
1	2,500	0.862	2,155	0.847	2,118	0.833	2,083
2	4,600	0.743	3,418	0.718	3,303	0.694	3,192
3	5,700	0.641	3,654	0.609	3,471	0.571	3,255
4	7,000	0.552	3,864	0.516	3,612	0.482	3,374

Present Value	13,091	12,504	11,904
Deduct cost	12,500	12,500	12,500
Net Present Value	591	4	596

The maximum rate of interest the company should pay to finance the project is 18 per cent, since, when discounted at this rate, the NPV of the project's cash flows approaches zero. If a greater rate is paid, the project's NPV becomes negative – and therefore unacceptable: at 20 per cent the NPV becomes –£596.

A TUTOR'S ANSWER

4

(a) The weighted cost of each type of capital is merely the cost of each type multiplied by its relative importance within the total capital structure. With ordinary shares, therefore, the cost is 20 per cent, and ordinary shares make up 50 per cent of the total amount of capital. The weighted cost is thus $20 \times 50 = 1,000$.

The cost of debentures has to be amended to allow for the after-tax cost. By applying the formula $r = R(1-t)$, we obtain: 10 per cent $(1-0.4) = 10$ per cent $\times 0.6 = 6$ per cent.

Type of finance	Return (%)	Amount (£000)	Weight	Weight × cost
Ord. shares	20	1,000	50	1,000
Pref. shares	16	600	30	480
Debentures	6	400	20	120
			100	1,600

Weighted average cost of capital $= \dfrac{1600}{100} = 16\%$

(b) (ii) Under payback, the projects are ranked:

Arrow   2 years
Spear   2½ years
Dart   3 years

(b) (ii) When using the NPV approach, it is necessary to discount the estimated cash flows by the discount factors. The discounted cash flows are then totalled, and the original cost is deducted. Any project giving a positive NPV is acceptable.

Year	Discount factor	Arrow		Dart		Spear	
1	0.862	7,000 =	6,034	6,500 =	5,603	8,200 =	7,068.4
2	0.743	11,000 =	8,173	7,000 =	5,201	10,400 =	7,727.2
3	0.641	11,300 =	7,243.3	8,500 =	5,448.5	10,800 =	6,922.8
4	0.552	11,500 =	6,348	12,800 =	7,065.6	11,600 =	6,403.2
5	0.476	11,900 =	5,664.4	14,300 =	6,806.8	12,000 =	5,712.2
Present Value			33,462.7		30,124.9		33,833.6
Less cost			18,000		22,000		24,000
Net Present Value			15,462.7		8,124.9		9,833.6

Using NPV, the projects are ranked: Spear, Arrow, and Dart. When using NPV, projects with higher NPVs are preferred to those with lower NPVs.

(c) It is likely that the examiner will accept an answer based upon either method, provided that a sufficiently strong case is argued in its support. With payback, although the time value of money is ignored, it is often argued that NPV depends so much upon different assumptions that the worth of the approach is more apparent than real. By accepting those projects that payback quickly, undue risk is avoided, and so too is the trouble of elaborate risk calculations.

NPV does allow for time values, and it takes account of cash flows well after the payback period. The method is, however, dependent upon assumptions about future costs of capital, and the likelihood of net cash flows being realised.

A STEP FURTHER

Arnold and Hope, *Accounting For Management Decisions*. Prentice Hall, Chs 4, 5, 12 and 13.

Daff, *Cost and Management Accounting*. Woodhead Faulkner, Ch. 9.

Drury, *Management and Cost Accounting*. Van Nostrand Reinhold, Chs 13 and 14.

Harvey and Nettleton, *Management Accounting*. Mitchell Beazley, Ch. 6.

Lucey, *Costing*. D. P. Publications, Ch. 22.

Lucey, *Management Accounting*. D. P. Publications, Chs 18 and 19.

Index

cost, 20
profit,
    graph, 127–8
    sharing schemes, 49
    uncompleted contracts, 86
pro-forma invoice, 30
purchase invoice, 30
purchase order, 30
purchase requisition, 30

rectification, 76, 80–1
re-order,
    levels, 32, 37
    quantity, 32, 37
retention money, 86–7
risk, 180–2
Rowan scheme, 48

salaries, 45
sales,
    budgets, 147
    invoice, 30
    order, 30
scrap, 101
semi-variable costs, 37, 42
separation point, 105, 109
service,
    cost account, 117, 119–21
    cost centre, 20
    costing, 73, 116–22
    departments' overheads, 58–61, 65
specific order costing, 73
split-off point, 105, 109
spreadsheets, 35
SSAP 9, 33, 86, 91–2, 98, 124, 144
standard,
    costing, 153, 158–73
    hour, 161
    setting, 158–9, 168
stock,
    control, 28–9, 35–6, 38–9,
    obsolescent, 37
    physical issues, 33
    taking, 33–4, 36, 41

stockholding cost, 31
stockout cost, 31
storekeeping, 36
stores,
    control, 31–2
    procedure, 29–31
straight piece work, 47–8
sub-stores, 31
sunk costs, 130, 136

taxation, 177–8
time,
    keeping, 46
    rates, 47
    sheets, 46
    value of money, 175
true cost, 24

usage variance, 160, 165–6, 169–71

valuing,
    fixed assets, 176–7
    material issues, 32–33
variable,
    costs, 37, 41, 130, 132, 136
    overhead variances, 160–1, 167, 172–3
variance accounting, 104, 109, 164, 177–8
variances, 20, 158–9, 160–2
volume variance, 161, 167, 172

wages, 45–7
    efficiency variance, 164, 169
    rate variance, 160, 164, 169
    systems, 46–9
waste, 101
work-in-progress, 85, 102, 104, 106

yield, 175, 177, 180–3
    variance, 160

zero base budgeting, 148, 151, 154–5